FAMILY VALUE AT RISK

Building a legacy wealthier
than money!

JR GONDECK
VANESSA N. MARTINEZ

FAMILY VALUE

— AT —

RISK

INCLUSIVE COMMUNICATION TO PASS ON YOUR
FAMILY'S WEALTH AND LEGACY

ForbesBooks

Published by ForbesBooks, Charleston, South Carolina.
Member of Advantage Media Group.

ForbesBooks is a registered trademark, and the ForbesBooks colophon is a trademark of Forbes Media, LLC.

Printed in the United States of America.

10 9 8 7 6 5 4 3 2 1

ISBN: 978-1-95086-316-7
LCCN: 2020912141

Cover design by George Stevens.
Layout design by Carly Blake.

This custom publication is intended to provide accurate information and the opinions of the author in regard to the subject matter covered. It is sold with the understanding that the publisher, Advantage|ForbesBooks, is not engaged in rendering legal, financial, or professional services of any kind. If legal advice or other expert assistance is required, the reader is advised to seek the services of a competent professional.

Advantage Media Group is proud to be a part of the Tree Neutral® program. Tree Neutral offsets the number of trees consumed in the production and printing of this book by taking proactive steps such as planting trees in direct proportion to the number of trees used to print books. To learn more about Tree Neutral, please visit **www.treeneutral.com**.

Since 1917, Forbes has remained steadfast in its mission to serve as the defining voice of entrepreneurial capitalism. ForbesBooks, launched in 2016 through a partnership with Advantage Media Group, furthers that aim by helping business and thought leaders bring their stories, passion, and knowledge to the forefront in custom books. Opinions expressed by ForbesBooks authors are their own. To be considered for publication, please visit **www.forbesbooks.com**.

This book, and honestly where we both are today,
would not have been possible without our family!

JR and I are strong believers that family consists of
people you care for and care about—those who need you
and, most importantly, you need.

Thank you to our families at home and at work and the
families who have shared their experiences with us!

CONTENTS

INTRODUCTION FROM THE COAUTHORS

Your wealth is more than just your money. Your wealth is your family, your legacy, and the future of the people, communities, and causes you love.

If you manage only your family's *money* and don't prioritize your overall wealth, then you are putting your family value—all the wealth derived from the aspects of life that are most important to you—at risk.

We wrote this book to review these risks and share our solutions, which we describe as our *Family Value at Risk*, or FVR, approach to wealth management. Our approach is a response to—and remedy for—two significant trends we have experienced in recent years.

First, we have seen how a narrow focus on investment returns by advisors and investors alike has come at the expense of a family's overall wealth. We know there is more to wealth beyond the ROI (return on investment). For example, investment returns can steadily earn an individual and their family considerable wealth. However, if there is not a coordinated plan in place as to how to distribute that money upon the individual's death, a substantial tax bill may reduce that wealth overnight.

Second, society has evolved to become more inclusive. We see this trend in education and employment across almost every industry. More women than ever are working in what were traditionally male-centric industries, such as finance, and bringing with them a fresh perspective that has the potential to drive positive change. At the same time, more women are stepping into the role of the primary bread-winner and financial decision maker. However, 49 percent of married women still let their spouse take the lead in financial planning.[1]

Wealth advisors must respond to the change. They have to understand that their approach must focus on the whole family, not just the traditional head of household.

Today, we recognize the benefits of inclusion even more than we did a generation ago. Going forward, we believe a more inclusive and collaborative approach to a family's wealth can be of tremendous benefit to our clients, our industry, and society at large.

We work in wealth advising because we are deeply passionate about helping families successfully grow, manage, and transfer wealth for generations to come. That passion extends beyond investment returns and into managing a family's assets, estate, legacy, and everything that comprises the family's overall wealth.

We also believe in a partnership approach, typically a team comprised of a male and female advisor who meet with both spouses. Why? Because an inclusive, balanced approach to wealth management consistently achieves stronger outcomes for everyone. It is part of why we are such strong advocates for more female representation in the finance industry.

We know firsthand that if clients and advisors shift from being

---

1   Nick Fortuna, "More Married Women Want to Take Bigger Part in Household Financial Planning, Survey Shows," Barron's, July 4, 2020, https://www.barrons.com/articles/more-married-women-want-to-take-bigger-part-in-household-financial-planning-survey-shows-51593864001.

investment centric to focusing on family dynamics and embrace *inclusivity*, families can achieve a greater degree of prosperity and harmony in managing their wealth.

As partners of Chicago-based wealth management firm the Lerner Group with HighTower Advisors, our team manages over $1.4 billion in assets as of 2020. This number is actually tripled when accounting for the advice we give families on their additional assets, such as real estate, insurance, private business income, alternative investments, and foundations.

We mention this larger number because most financial metrics prioritize assets under management, ignoring other forms of family wealth. We see an opportunity in expanding not only what we manage but also how we fundamentally track wealth metrics in our industry. Traditional financial advisors have the reputation of focusing only on the assets they are paid to manage. If the asset is not "billable," it won't make it into their planning process and isn't likely to be part of the total wealth plan they create for families. After working with hundreds of client families for decades, we know billable assets are inseparable from other forms of value when it comes to prioritizing a family's wealth and future.

As you read on, know that we wrote this book to educate you on why the greatest *risk* to a family's wealth and legacy is the status quo approach to managing money. We hope you enjoy learning how an FVR approach can help pass your family's wealth and legacy for generations to come.

> The greatest *risk* to a family's wealth and legacy is the status quo approach to managing money.

OUR APPROACH: ON PARTNERSHIPS AND RISK

Most of our clients are couples who are growing their wealth for retirement and to effectively pass it on to their children, grandchildren, and the communities and causes they love. That is at odds with a long-standing reality of the financial industry, which has—until recently—been under the purview of men: male advisors and male clients.

As a whole, the industry has been slower to adapt to changes happening elsewhere in society. Excluding input from or involvement with female advisors, female clients, or clients' female family members can have inherent risks.

For one, the life span of a male is typically shorter than that of his female partner. While this fact may seem morbid, it matters for many families—particularly when it comes to wealth planning. With the knowledge that most women will outlive their male partners, we must involve the spouse *equally* in all financial planning and decision-making. Doing otherwise, as we've seen, can have disastrous results for families and prevent the optimal transfer of wealth.

For example, here's a scenario we've watched unfold time and again: A husband accumulates a good deal of money, works with a male advisor on further investing and planning, and rarely speaks with his wife about any of their family's financial details. Then, the husband passes away, and the new widow is forced to play catch-up on hundreds of details and make costly decisions—most of which could have been avoided had her husband and advisor included her in the planning process. She struggles to preserve what she has and is potentially forced to revise the plan last minute, all while dealing with the grief of her husband's passing. She is left to wonder whether the responsibility to be better prepared was hers, her husband's, or her advisor's.

But that's not the only risk involved in traditional wealth

planning. Another risk stems from the typical focus of advisors and clients on investment returns. A client's most important question has always seemed to be, "How much money can I accumulate?"

At first glance you'd think the right equation would be *more money=better for everybody*. But we've seen hundreds, if not *thousands*, of circumstances in which chasing returns has had a net *negative* effect on the family's overall wealth. There is risk to long-term wealth when the focus is on chasing returns and not prioritizing the family's future. To avoid as many of these negative effects as possible, we developed a more inclusive approach.

Our FVR approach involves spouses, children, and all concerned parties in the wealth-planning process. Over the years, we've discovered that the more you involve spouses, children, other family members, and related parties in the wealth-planning process, the more the question of "how much" becomes secondary. Instead, people begin to ask, "Given our resources, how can we do what's best for our family and our future?"

This inclusivity makes investment returns less of a concern from the beginning. With men and women playing a collaborative role, the focus first and foremost rests on overall family wealth, harmony, and values. In our approach, the money and returns become a means to an end, rather than the entire goal.

OUR MISSION

As a family wealth advisor, JR has experienced both ends of the spectrum: the traditional, status quo approach and the FVR approach. These experiences make him an advocate of the latter. He has seen how it can be far more successful in the long term, facilitating both the preservation and transfer of wealth.

JR'S TAKE

My goal in writing this book is to change the mindset of both families and the industry as a whole. We shouldn't be laser-focused only on investment returns. Instead, we encourage inclusive planning and decision-making.

We should educate couples, helping prepare them for the reality that men often don't live as long as women do. With that in mind, the more prepared all parties are, the more likely it is that the family's wealth and values will pass to the next generation.

We should break down the old way of looking at investments. Going forward, our role should be to fully educate families, so they can carry on their legacy, bringing stability to their wealth for generations to come.

I've experienced the old way—investing and advising without much collaborative involvement from both spouses. I've experienced the way it can be when each spouse has an equal role in navigating their financial matters. The old way wasn't necessarily all bad. However, in living through both, I've seen that the new way is a material improvement—in terms of taking care of families long term and establishing a more stable and secure financial future.

Coauthor and partner at the Lerner Group, Vanessa, also understands that a more inclusive wealth planning experience produces better outcomes for families.

VANESSA'S TAKE

My purpose in writing this book is to share with others what I've learned from both the good and the bad of the traditional approach to wealth management. I want to help educate families about a more inclusive way to make stronger financial decisions. I can't meet with every family around the world, so this book is my attempt to spread our message further than I could ever physically reach.

More people need to hear about the results derived from this approach. If by reading this book, you learn from the FVR approach and are able to apply at least one aspect to your family, then we've succeeded.

This book should help you understand how wealth has evolved—today, we *shouldn't* think it's just about the money. It's about so much more. And the more we share our approach, the more opportunity we all have. I truly believe that if we promote this message and demonstrate its value over and over again, people will experience its incredible benefits.

Being a woman in the world—not just in this industry— and having navigated my way through different obstacles and adversities, I'm proud to use my experience to help others experience something *better*. I'm now in a position where I can lead, where I can make my voice heard. I want to use it to help as many families as possible.

OUR JOURNEY: WHY WE WROTE *FAMILY VALUE AT RISK* FOR YOU

When Vanessa says it's been a fight to get where we are today, she's not exaggerating. Our journey hasn't always been easy, but seeing where we are today, it's one for which we are deeply thankful.

In the pages ahead, you'll get better acquainted with us, our clients, yourself, and your family's wealth situation. Before we dive in, we'd like to tell you a bit more about who we are, how we arrived at the conclusions we describe in this book, and why we are so passionate about the work we do.

JR'S JOURNEY

I grew up in a lower-middle-class home in northern Wisconsin, just north of Green Bay. As one of five boys, I did my part to contribute. I started making money in first grade, when I had a paper route. The first time I earned twenty dollars, I thought I was the richest person in the world. My mother raised me to be very independent and self-sufficient. For a long time, I interpreted those responsibilities to mean money should motivate me and my decision-making process more than anything else.

I worked all through high school on a farm, milking cows at 4:30 a.m. and then again after school. From there I went to college at Marquette University in Milwaukee, Wisconsin. At first, I studied engineering, because I had always enjoyed math and science. But I quickly learned that finance was my calling.

I switched my major to finance after my freshman year. I can still remember walking down Wisconsin Avenue, making the move from the engineering school to the business school. It was a life-changing moment, and I never looked back. While I was in school, I worked full time at a bank. I was able to graduate a semester early and move to Chicago.

I was sleeping on my brother's couch while searching for a job. It took me a little over a month to find employment, but it felt like the longest month of my life. Finally, I found a job with Morgan Stanley.

At the time, Morgan Stanley was hiring only temps, due to a hiring freeze. So I took a temporary position with Eugene Lerner's team, where I officially did research but unofficially spent most of my time just listening. Little did I know that Gene would become my greatest mentor. Gene was a giant in finance. He studied under famed economist Milton Friedman at the University of Chicago. This is where he received his doctorate and later became a professor, teaching pupils including future Federal Reserve Chairman Alan Greenspan.

I felt fortunate to have a mentor with such a distinguished pedigree, and I wanted to soak up as much knowledge as possible. Once the hiring freeze was over, I became a full-time financial advisor, starting formally in the business at twenty-one. I worked, listened, worked some more, and listened some more. After some time, Gene began to trust me to make decisions, and we grew the business from there.

When Gene founded the business in the early 1970s, he was a pioneer in using computers to help pick stocks, employing rules-based algorithms to help advisors scan through thousands of companies to design portfolios.

During my first five years, we grew the business fivefold—until the 2008 financial crisis hit. As it did with many businesses, the Great Recession changed ours forever. By the bottom of the market in March 2009, our business had been reduced by nearly half its size from the previous year. What had primarily been an equity-based firm evolved into one with a more diversified strategy, with individual bonds and individual stocks to generate the balance that families needed to ride out the ups and downs of the market.

By then, my personal situation had changed as well. In 2008, I started business school at Northwestern's Kellogg School of Management in Evanston, Illinois—a two-year MBA program that took me nearly four years to finish, primarily because of the market and business turmoil.

During this period, many of our clients also experienced significant life changes—several that we were ill-prepared to manage. Most of our clients were from older generations. Though they had achieved significant wealth over the course of their lifetimes, they hadn't necessarily taken steps to preserve their wealth. We found that clients had rarely reached out to their attorneys to review and revise their documents and, in most cases, had an estate plan that was many years expired. Death is an uncomfortable topic, and we have found that, because of this, families were hesitant to stay on top of their estate plans. Due to the transactional nature of the industry, many attorneys were reactive rather than proactive, which meant they weren't driving the conversation.

In addition, in the majority of our meetings, we met only with the patriarch of the family—in those times, the primary breadwinner and decision maker. Typically, the patriarch trusted us and assumed or requested that we would take care of his spouse and family when he passed. As a result, in many cases, when the patriarch passed away, the spouse either didn't know the plan or was not prepared to make complicated financial decisions alone. These last-minute decisions inherently created significant expenses that could have been avoided had she been involved in the coordination of financial affairs before his passing.

After watching numerous cases like this unfold, I finally learned a key lesson: money *isn't* everything. Its greatest use is in serving as a tool to help people. As we often say: money is a means and not an end. That belief guides us to this day.

Gene and I spent ten years at Morgan Stanley and then transitioned to HighTower in 2012. We left a big firm for an independent one. At HighTower, our team is no longer tethered to big firm conventions and mechanics. Today

> **Money is a means and not an end. That belief guides us to this day.**

we operate without a top-down wealth-planning approach or an overarching goal designed to benefit the firm's bottom line rather than our clients. As such, we have the advantage of being able to put clients first and serve them the best way we know how.

Within a couple of years after moving to HighTower, Gene phased out of the day-to-day business. Vanessa joined our team during this period, and I found myself in a state similar to when I first joined Gene—I was mostly listening and soaking up as much insight and knowledge as I could.

As a woman, Vanessa brought a totally different dynamic and perspective to the Lerner Group, one that was somewhat foreign to me as a financial professional. She was a total game changer.

I began to learn just how much I didn't know—and how important it was to consider the impact of our decisions on the whole family. With my vigor renewed, Vanessa and I began addressing our client offerings, how we would provide them and why. From the moment she joined the team, our client service philosophy began evolving to where it is today.

I found the balance of different views—mostly the differences between typical male and female considerations—to be eye opening. It was transformative from a business perspective and in terms of how it changed the dynamic of client meetings. With Vanessa's guidance, we encouraged more meetings including both spouses and approached them as a partnership ourselves.

The questions and discussion that Vanessa thought to ask and/or touch on were areas I wasn't typically comfortable with. But once these important issues were on the table, everyone felt more comfortable discussing them and we were able to create better outcomes for everyone. This collaborative dynamic allowed us to resolve challenges that had once been tremendously difficult to unearth—let alone address. For the first time, I saw that communication and balance of views both within the industry and within families is critically important.

Today, Vanessa and I take seriously our responsibility to introduce our FVR approach. We serve as the primary family wealth advisor for complex modern family office clients. Our work is vitally important to us, and we both understand that with our shared knowledge, it is up to us to not only continue to better serve our clients but also to evolve the industry's traditional approach. And that starts with sharing our message in this book.

VANESSA'S JOURNEY

My father is from El Salvador, and my mother is from Guatemala; they met in Chicago, where my two sisters and I were born and raised. When I was seven, my father began working for American Airlines. Every summer, the day after the school year ended, we would fly to Guatemala and stay until September when school started again.

Over the years I became attached to Guatemala, its culture, and its people. I fell so much in love with the country that I knew when I graduated from high school, I would go there for college. My youthful certainty led me to skip taking the SATs, as the test is not required in Guatemala.

Traveling back and forth gave me a different perspective on money and its impact. Seeing the poverty and pain of other people struggling to provide for their families, I gained an appreciation for the prosperity that we have here in the US. I could no longer throw away a pair of shoes that still had life in them or fail to finish the food on my plate with the knowledge that there were so many who didn't take those things for granted.

Giving back to others became my most powerful motivator. I wanted to use my understanding and abilities to change lives for the better. I continue to believe that I should always give back—regardless of how much I have. I believe each of us should give from our hearts rather than just sharing what we have left over.

While living in Guatemala, I worked full time for a lumber manufacturing company as the international sales manager. This allowed me to be self-sufficient and pay for college. Whether by fate or happy accident, this job gave me the opportunity to forge my own path to success. I was able to define myself as a professional and tackle the challenges of being a woman in a traditionally male-dominated industry.

The company employed five hundred individuals, only four of whom were women: one quality control officer, one chef, a front-desk receptionist, and me. They first brought me in as an assistant to the production manager due to the language barrier they encountered with their international clients.

After three months of building out a full schedule and plan on the machinery, I became so closely involved with the clients and established such great relationships that I earned the position of international sales manager. This was a defining opportunity, as I started traveling to Germany, the US, and Canada. On one of the trips, we even created a joint venture.

At first, I encountered resistance. It was difficult to be taken seriously in a room full of men. I had to outshine and outperform others around me just to have the opportunity to be heard. But I knew my value, and I was diligent in my pursuit of personal and professional betterment and success.

Then, a decade ago, I was in one of my final business classes, sitting in a sweltering room with no air conditioning and listening to my professor talk about how *making the right financial decisions today is critical to our future success.* It was there, in that stuffy little room filled with fellow undergrads, that I realized what I wanted to do with my life.

My professor said making the right decisions today helps us succeed tomorrow—I wanted not only to make the right financial decisions for myself and for my family but also to help others do the same. It was then that I decided to start pursuing my passion and purpose by directing my focus to finance.

With my undergraduate degree in hand, I returned to Chicago and enrolled in an MBA program. While in graduate school at North Park University, I started gaining experience in the field by working at JPMorgan Chase as a personal banker and then as a branch manager.

In 2013, I joined the Lerner Group as a client service manager. In just over a year, I became the chief operating officer. This was due to my passion for strategic planning and business development. By helping establish future plans for the firm, I demonstrated the value of my contributions to the partners and earned my promotion.

As COO, I worked with the team to negotiate contracts, transition to a new custodian, reinvigorate team culture, and establish a career-development program. We created a full wealth-planning road map.

Encouraging the team to adopt the concept of a more collaborative family approach to wealth planning became my true end goal, and the team rallied around this push. These contributions elevated me to a partnership role within three years.

I was blessed to work with partners who were able to appreciate my guidance, empowered me daily, and welcomed modern ideas. JR and Ming (fellow HighTower partner) are truly great listeners. As JR mentioned, he was able to listen to everything Gene had to say, understand it, and then pass it on. JR was able to learn money and client management from a master. When Gene retired, JR then became the speaker and not the listener, the teacher and not the student.

From that point on, JR realized the needs of clients were changing and the financial industry was not addressing them. Clients weren't just concerned about their stocks and investment returns. They were discussing topics including properties, assets, relationships, deaths, births, titles, wills, trusts, legacy, and so much more—all of which have a direct impact on one's wealth. JR was fully listening to all their needs.

JR and I both recognized the need not only to include spouses in the meetings but also to have another advisor in the room. Doing so allows for deeper discovery with the family. A two-person advisor team, comprised of both male and female advisors, allows for more in-depth discussions.

When we work as a team communicating with couples, we know our roles and how each of us can advance the conversation. We know when to listen, when to talk, when to bring in others, and when to move on. In the work we do, having emotional intelligence is a gift.

Driven by passion, willing to take risks, and having learned to make decisions early, JR and I are very proud of how far we've come, where we are today, and where we are headed. We both continue to listen, learn, lead, grow, and give.

OUR GOAL FOR YOUR FAMILY AND THE FUTURE OF WEALTH PLANNING

Family Value at Risk is a call to action for clients like you and the financial industry as a whole. We must wake up to the fact that the less inclusive, status quo approach to investing and wealth management creates large gaps in the process, which can be detrimental to the future of your family's wealth.

Why are most investors and advisors so focused on money and investment returns? Why do they spend virtually no time working on everything else that affects your family's wealth?

This book is for families and industry professionals who see the benefits in expanding the traditional approach to wealth to include family values and dynamics.

We all agree that society is changing and we need to meet its developing needs. This book is our attempt to rally together clients and the industry so that our concept of value and how we manage wealth evolves in step with our changing society.

With shifting societal dynamics in mind, this book serves numerous readers—each with a different perspective but the same ultimate goal: to successfully pass on or inherit wealth.

Whether your goal is to support a cause you care deeply about or to provide for your family—be it a spouse, your children, members of a blended family, grandchildren, or even great-grandchildren—you will undoubtedly uncover insights that will help you achieve your objective. Let's dig a little deeper into the types of readers served here:

- "Matriarchs" or "patriarchs," those family leaders looking for tips on how to share their wealth and legacy with future generations.

- Blended families interested in hearing stories on successful legacy planning.

- Individual wealth creators looking for guidance on how to pass on an inheritance.

- Those navigating the challenge of gifting in a manner that is fair versus equal.

- Those who will be inheriting a gift and want to ensure they are not compromising current or future wealth in the process.

Regardless of your circumstances, we believe the stories shared in this book can help your family learn and make changes where necessary or maybe just confirm you are already on the right path!

Before we get started, we would like to share a note on structure. We wrote this book as coauthors to mirror our collaborative partnership when advising clients. We will each present a few chapters from our individual perspective. Within these chapters, the other coauthor contributes a few quotes, stories, and takeaways. The conclusion is presented by both of us.

Together, we have compiled our experience and expertise into an easy-to-read guide, explaining why and how families benefit from an enhanced approach to managing their wealth. Here, you'll learn about

- how we work with husbands, wives, and children to do what is best for families,

- asset management, including how our Family Value at Risk, or FVR, approach applies to concentration and diversification,

- estate planning solutions, including how to approach titles and probate,

- legacy planning solutions that account for your unique family dynamics and values, and

- how to overcome the decision-making paralysis that comes from a lack of guidance and limited options.

You and your family are on a journey together. If you're concerned that your family's legacy is potentially at risk, know that there are other solutions—and that we'll identify some of them here.

By the end of the book, you should be confident that you have a useful guide you can reference as you pursue asset, estate, and legacy planning. With our FVR approach by your side, you are ready to prioritize your family's wealth and legacy.

CHAPTER 1

FAMILY VALUE AT RISK

In chapter 1, Vanessa shares an all-too-common story of family adversity. She demonstrates how a status quo approach to wealth can put your family value at risk. She also shares hope by introducing the comprehensive, family-friendly approach to wealth that can benefit us all.

Here is a sad story embodying the risk of damaged communication, one that happens every day. Yet, the fact that so many families experience it doesn't ever make it easier for anyone. That was certainly the case for Sabrina and her family.

I first became acquainted with Sabrina's situation a few years ago, when her brother, our client Aaron, mentioned her at the end of his portfolio review. With an urgent and uncharacteristically serious expression, Aaron asked us if we could help Sabrina, who lived in another city and was considering switching advisors. I told him I'd be happy to help, whatever the situation.

The next night, at approximately 7:30 p.m., I got a call on my cell phone while I was cooking dinner.

"Hi, Vanessa? This is Sabrina, Aaron's sister. I'm sorry it's so late. I know I shouldn't be calling you at this time."

"Don't think twice about it; I'm so glad you called!" I said. "I was expecting to hear from you. Your brother mentioned you needed some guidance?" I asked, handing the spatula to my husband.

"My husband's in the hospital. He's been diagnosed with advanced pancreatic cancer. I don't know what to do."

"I'm so sorry," I said. "I can't imagine all the thoughts running through your mind right now. Please tell me what I can do to help."

She hesitated, as many do when first discussing their family's financial situation with a new advisor. Then, after a long pause, she broke down. "He's dying. He's dying!" she said between sobs. "The doctors say he has six months to live—at best. We have two adult children together, and he has a son from his first marriage. I really don't know if I or our children will have enough money when … "

She was not able to finish her sentence.

Having worked with her brother, Aaron, I had assumed that Sabrina had received a modest inheritance from her deceased parents, just as he had. When I asked about it, Sabrina replied, "I spent some of it on his medical expenses. But even more than just the money—I'm overwhelmed and confused. I'm very unorganized, and I don't under-stand what to do about our finances. Could you give me some type of list so I can feel like I am checking off things to do?"

"Of course," I said. I began asking her questions to help build a critical to-do list. We talked for an hour and got to know one another. By the end of the call, I heard her sigh with relief.

"I feel so comfortable with you," she said. "I typically wouldn't make a quick decision like this, but you are asking questions that others haven't, and I can see that you have a more holistic view on my family.

I'd feel so much better about my situation with you guiding me."

"We'll do everything we can to help make sure things are in order," I said.

Over the next few weeks, we worked together to check off the boxes. At the same time, her husband's condition quickly deteriorated.

Within a week of our first call, Sabrina called me again out of the blue, in tears. "Vanessa, he's coming home. They don't have anything else they can do for him in the hospital. His mind is gone. They say he has at most a few months."

She talked about in-home care: hiring a part-time nurse and looking after him the rest of the time on her own. She contemplated the options for the right end-of-life support he would need to ensure his comfort. At the same time, she had bills to pay and household tasks to complete. She seemed lost, forced to make decision after decision in the worst possible moment, when she was overwhelmed with grief.

As the days passed, she'd often call looking for guidance. "I don't know what to do now. I can't do this. I don't care if I spend all my money; I'm going to get a full-time health provider. I have to." We worked through her options, and I gave her my team's best recommendations.

Meanwhile, we worked to set up her family's estate and assets to protect their wealth from probate. Whatever assets were titled in his individual name, we retitled into joint ownership. Real estate, private business-related assets, investment accounts, and more. He did not have a list of his assets, so we prayed we were able to account for every last one.

After just a month, I received the news that he had passed away. We gave Sabrina a couple of weeks after he passed, then JR and I flew to visit her.

We spent the whole day with her and her two adult children. It felt so good to meet them in person, to give her a hug and tell her, "It's okay; you did everything you could," and to reassure her that we were still here to help. She expressed her gratitude for our unwavering support.

While we took care of as much as we could for her in the short time we had, we knew from the beginning that if she had called a year or even six months earlier, we could've avoided some losses and protected so much more.

As is the case with many married couples, Sabrina's husband managed the finances and communicated the bare minimum to her. That meant that while she told us about every asset she readily knew of, *those only represented a portion of what her husband owned.*

It was a precarious situation, and it came to a head a short time after his passing, when Sabrina received a stack of boxes from her husband's office. Sorting through the piles, she found documents that made her stomach drop. First, she found a deed for a condo in Hilton Head, South Carolina. When a property is held in deed form, the owner must sign off on it, which was now impossible. She also found a car in his name being leased for his son. Since the lease wasn't retitled ahead of time, the car was repossessed because no action was taken.

Back when we had reviewed all the family assets, we asked her again and again, "Is there anything else that you are aware of?"

"No," she'd say. "I don't have anything else."

"Are you sure?"

Everyone's answer, of course, is, "Yeah, I'm sure. I don't have anything else … that I know of."

In situations like Sabrina's, we do as much as possible, as early as possible, to prioritize objectives and options for the family's wealth and future. Unfortunately, we know all too well what happens when we're too late.

What motivates me every day—and what motivated JR and me to write this book—is to help families avoid situations like Sabrina's. Her story is all too common. I wish more than anything that Sabrina's story would be the last of its kind, that such misfortune would never again befall any spouse or family. The lack of inclusive and intentional communication between spouses is a trend that continues today. What we need is for husbands to communicate better with their wives, and in addition, we need the wives to promote the conversation by asking more questions.

WHY IS OUR FAMILY VALUE AT RISK?

In the earlier part of my financial career, I attended many events where I socialized with couples. Most times, once the couple found out I was a banker, the husband would start chatting about his investments and the wife would visibly shut down. I could see the pain on her face as she would listen silently to the discussion, feeling either that it wasn't her place to comment or that she was too embarrassed due to her lack of knowledge about the subjects discussed.

"Don't worry," the husband would often say to me with a wink, "I'll explain it to her later." Not only are comments like that unnecessary, they are incredibly detrimental to the family's wealth. Wouldn't it be so much better if the spouse were equally informed? Isn't it likely the spouse could be just as capable of stewarding the family's wealth—if not more so—as statistically it's more likely the husband will die before her?

At first, I'd nod along, not doing much in the moment to help educate the spouse. I understood our society's financial culture had long been the domain of men. A part of me accepted that, unwillingly.

But today, I just can't accept it.

Over the years, I've sat through too many meetings with grieving widows who don't understand the first thing about their family's financial future.

After a spouse's death, women like Sabrina sit and cry with me, telling me they have no idea what to do next. It's heartbreaking to know that they're trying to mourn, but they can't fully grieve because they don't know what they'll do tomorrow or when their next bill needs to be paid. This is the catalyst I needed to help motivate families to have inclusive communication between spouses. I understand that this will take an adoption period, but it must start somewhere.

WOMEN: WE ARE OUR OWN BEST ADVOCATE

In the past, it was common for women to be disengaged when it came to the ins and outs of their financial options. Financial planning was mostly the domain of husbands and male advisors.

Today, society has shifted, and more women are creating and taking responsibility for their overall wealth. Now, we must participate in our own financial future. Like many women, I believe we must take on the responsibility of educating ourselves. We cannot depend entirely on our spouses to teach us what we need to know.

We have so many resources today that were not available to previous generations, such as the internet, financial seminars, and female wealth advisors like me and the women on the team. We must utilize these resources to maximize our understanding so we can better manage our wealth with our partners and on our own.

As women, we can sometimes feel a little intimidated by certain people, and sadly, sometimes our own husbands can be among them. That could mean we don't confide in that person as a resource when we need more information or the comfort level hasn't been built.

I want women to know they can count on me personally, as a woman, and on our team as a whole. If you are unsure about what something means, or what to do about it, you never have to feel dumb asking questions. As advisors, we are here to educate. We didn't always have the answers. We've had to learn over time. We're still learning every day, and we can help others do the same.

What we cannot do is accept the status quo, because acceptance comes with the risks we describe in this book. Instead, we must learn to be our own advocate.

Confused and confronted with countless decisions and forced to make those decisions at the worst possible time and without the years of experience and guidance their husbands received from participating in the family's wealth management, they feel like the questions never end. How do I pay a bill? Will we have enough to live on? How do I make sense of our family's situation?

In those low moments, it's especially difficult for spouses to trust my guidance, because they've only talked to me a handful of times. We might have spoken at an event or simply exchanged greetings before she passed the phone to their husband when I returned his call.

This painful scenario is endemic in our financial industry. It's one experienced by many families.

In the chapters ahead, we showcase our Family Value at Risk, or FVR, approach to wealth management. It is a deeper, more inclusive way for families to plan and manage their wealth, one that accounts for the greatest risk to long-term family value: the financial industry's traditional strategies to manage wealth.

To further define Family Value at Risk and how it applies to you, let's break down the phrase.

FAMILY

Family to us is like the word *love*. It's a strong word, but its simplicity occasionally belies its meaning. To us, it doesn't just refer to bloodline. For instance, I feel the definition of family ties into my work, our team, and the families we serve as advisors. I also have many causes and communities that I love and consider a part of my family in one way or another. When people say "family," all the people and things I love is what comes to mind.

When I'm in a meeting or at brunch with clients, I can relate to their feelings when they talk about their family. I feel their pain when they discuss the disappointments and adversity they have experienced, and I share their happiness when they describe what brings them joy. Such an understanding of family dynamics—and all the accompanying joys and sorrows—allows us to grow closer to one another. Such a closeness helps give my team and me a more comprehensive and holistic understanding of not only their finances but also their realities, goals, and dreams.

FAMILY VALUE

JR and I find it hard to separate a family's investment side—everything that has to do with their money—from the family side—growth, understanding, love, and sharing of values. Family values are what drive a family's decisions, financial ones included.

A family's value isn't just defined by money and assets. Wealth is your family, your legacy, and the future of the people, communities, and causes you care about. If you value love, education, growth, hard work, relationships, or any such values, then those should define how you and your family approach your financial decision-making.

FAMILY VALUE AT RISK

In the traditional approach to family wealth, there's typically a family patriarch or matriarch who is both the primary breadwinner and decision maker. This individual has accrued a significant amount of wealth and assets, and he or she decides how to pass it on or not.

Our firm has worked with the same families for decades, allowing us to build relationships with multiple generations. For many of those families, the original patriarch or matriarch has passed long ago, and today we work with their grandchildren, great-grandchildren, and great-great-grandchildren.

What we've learned over the years is that if a financial plan is built with just one spouse or one generation in mind, it will eventually fail. After a generation or two, the wealth will disappear, financial and otherwise, if there isn't a focus on all three aspects of wealth: estate, asset, and legacy planning.

Today, we work with more than just the patriarch or matriarch. We work with spouses, children, and all current and future parties. Inclusivity, equal education, transparency—these principles help families preserve wealth, values, and everything the family holds dear. Without this approach, we've seen wealth surrender to risk.

JR'S DEFINITION OF
FAMILY VALUE AT RISK

From my background in investing, "risk" was always a financial term used to describe the potential volatility of investments in a portfolio. It accounted for how much of the investment could be "comfortably" lost in a volatile period. For example: a higher risk investment may gain 20 percent in a good year—but it could also depreciate 20 percent of your principal on a bad day.

As portfolio managers, we tracked many risk metrics to make sure clients' investments meet their goals within their risk tolerance. Traditionally, we only focused on those metrics associated with their returns. But we found that wasn't enough.

Often, we achieved good returns, only to see the corresponding wealth lost later to other financial circumstances outside the investments we managed. They were avoidable circumstances, such as inefficient estate planning, uncoordinated gifting, legal or tax burdens, and financial planning that didn't account for titling, trusts, and charitable legacy, to name a few.

With our FVR approach, we track so much more than investment returns to account for all possible risks to your wealth. We realize our inclusive, holistic definition of wealth planning and risk extends beyond the traditional approach. But now is the time for us to make new traditions—it is in everyone's best interest.

TODAY'S OPPORTUNITY TO DO MORE THAN THE STATUS QUO

When we first work with a new family, the individuals we meet come to us having experienced only the status quo approach to managing wealth.

COSTLY FINANCIAL INDUSTRY AND WEALTH-PLANNING NORMS THAT NEED TO CHANGE:

- Focusing on investment returns and fees above all else

- Not including spouses, children, and all parties affected by financial decisions in any of the discussions about them

- Experiencing planning blind spots by ignoring the unique insights women bring to the table

- Not understanding that, statistically, men die earlier than women, and this has a huge impact on family value and financial planning success

- Leaving family values and non-return-based value considerations out of estate plans

- Not educating clients on all their wealth options

- Not making the complicated as simple as possible

- Waiting to make a decision until it's too late—i.e., decision-making paralysis

In the past, the norm was for advisors to simply follow a client's instructions. Clients would inform the advisor that they had a particular amount available to invest and ask about the strategy that would provide the best returns. Back then, we would have just taken the amount and invested it the best way we knew how. End of story.

But as you've learned already, times have changed, and our clients' needs and expectations for their wealth have evolved. We now have the opportunity to focus on more than just returns as we work with a family's full financial value, including insurance, properties, the private value of their business, investment accounts, college savings accounts, and other balances that can and should be accounted for.

> **By tracking overall *wealth*, we help families best manage their assets, structure their estates, and pass on their values and legacy.**

By tracking overall *wealth*, we help families best manage their assets, structure their estates, and pass on their values and legacy.

We have the opportunity to do it all. To avoid risk and best plan for and manage your wealth, we'll help you make the decisions that best serve you and your family.

DECISION-MAKING PARALYSIS

We have mentioned the phrase *decision-making paralysis* a couple of times already, but what does it really mean?

Decision-making paralysis may occur for a variety of reasons, from not understanding the situation at hand to not wanting to make the "wrong" decision. It's just human nature. When a decision presents itself as too complex and we're not able to comprehend it on our own, we tend to avoid it. We put off researching or consulting with an expert because it feels like a big task. And let's face it, we all have busy lives, with careers and families to attend to. Meanwhile, those daunting tasks keep getting kicked further and further down the line.

Other times, you may be torn by multiple options. For example, it's easy to become consumed with whether to gift to all your kids equally or to give more to those children who need it more.

That's where an advisor can be particularly helpful. While most people freeze on their own, saving the tough decision for another day, an advisor keeps you on track, helping you assess and avoid unnecessary risk.

WHAT TASKS ARE TYPICALLY AFFECTED BY DECISION-MAKING PARALYSIS?

- **Drafting a will and trust.** Why?
  - We don't like the expense of it, particularly the price tag.
  - We don't like to think about death and who takes over after.
  - We don't want to spend the time doing it when we have other pressing to-dos and death seems so far away.
- **Retitling.** Many of us avoid retitling the following accounts, which should be reviewed regularly:
  - Homes and other real estate
  - Private investments
  - Investment accounts
  - Bank accounts
- **Investing.** As a result, we tend to make the following mistakes:
  - Building up a savings account because we are nervous about making "the wrong" investment decision—and missing out on market moves in the process
  - Timing the market
  - Making the wrong decisions—or failing to make any decisions at all—about life insurance

WHAT ARE THE THREE LARGEST AREAS OF RISK FOR YOUR FAMILY'S WEALTH AND FUTURE?

When considering risk, there are three areas we help manage: estate, assets, and legacy. When we work with a family, we always consider the entire picture—including all three areas—when making decisions. With that said, families don't necessarily address all these topics at the same time. A growing family may need to address one more urgently than the others. For the purposes of this book, we'll explore these three areas in the order mentioned.

As discussed, our three-step approach is in contrast to that of the traditional industry. Typically, if investors only want to share liquid investable assets, advisors only advise on what they see. Both are doing a disservice to the investor's wealth. Our approach dives deeper, which has required us to have multiple in-house experts who allow us and our clients to break through the red tape and compile a full picture. Having these experts on our team means we have the ability to identify the right solutions and establish the best possible results for our clients. By working together, we can go the extra mile in doing what's best for each family.

But before we dive deeper into the benefits of this approach, let's talk about the risks accompanying a more limited focus.

I. YOUR ESTATE AT RISK

Risks to one's estate may be common—but that doesn't make them any less costly. Major risks include those we've seen in Sabrina's story, related to asset titling and probate. Adding to the risk is the reality that estate planning is complex. In addition to the fact that estate planning is unique to each family, every state has its own set of rules as to how estates may be handled.

Despite the complexity, people fall prey to most risks in the simplest way: by not reviewing their estate plans on a regular basis.

For example, some of you may have created a trust ten years ago. It's likely that, in the intervening years, your family has changed, situations have evolved, and what seemed like a good plan a decade ago will need updating. This is especially the case for trusts where the benefactor trustee has passed away, the family has experienced divorce, or any number of circumstances we see regularly in family dynamics. In addition, as they draft their estate plans, older generations often fail to coordinate with younger ones, which could be an expensive mistake, particularly for beneficiaries.

What is one way to reduce the risks associated with estate planning? Have a collaborative wealth advisor who is familiar with your estate plan recommend and integrate changes as your life evolves. We found that having an attorney/CPA on staff provides us with the ability to quickly review documents and make recommendations as necessary. This internal communication helps clients avoid the decision-making paralysis that occurs when a family needs to coordinate complex estate planning issues.

No one feels like they need an estate plan today. Nevertheless, unexpected life events inevitably occur—and that is why we need to plan for them now.

In chapters 2 and 3, we'll cover estate risks and solutions in greater detail. Having a plan in place early on saves a family future heartache and hardship. Keeping that plan updated, so that it accounts for all shifting legal, tax, and family dynamics, is essential to avoid risks that have affected so many.

II. YOUR ASSETS AT RISK

Your wealth includes your assets, such as investments, property, insurance, business income, and more. It may seem obvious that these items of value contribute to your wealth, but most families don't discuss all or even most of their investments with their financial advisor.

For example, let's consider the case of a typical entrepreneur running his business. Let's say he has $500,000 invested in stocks and another $500,000 in cash. Most advisors would track the return only on the portion that's invested with them, as opposed to the total sum, which could help improve the total financial picture.

On top of that, say the entrepreneur has a large amount of his net worth in a privately held business. When it comes to his risk profile, he'd likely want the asset investments to be a little more conservative, since he has enough risk accompanying the business. By accounting for the family's total assets, as opposed to only the investable liquid assets, there is more stability to that entrepreneur's wealth.

But more often than not, advisors don't have the internal expert to help handle every aspect of an investor's financial life. Due to the frequency of advisors trying to poach outside assets held with other firms, families tend to keep many of their outside investments private. It's understandable, but ultimately, the lack of transparency hinders success. Both advisors and investors are responsible for diving deep enough into a family's wealth to avoid risks.

While working with families, we don't necessarily need to manage all their wealth. We just have to be aware of how it's titled and the asset allocations so that we can best coordinate and ensure its enduring value.

We have also found that having a comprehensive view of all your assets in one place can not only be eye opening but also alleviate significant stress. We need to have the holistic view of your financial picture to be able to give you the best possible recommendation.

Having a simplified net worth statement allows us to prepare a visual of all your assets on one page, helping us manage the location of assets, their diversification, and income planning. What do we mean by that?

Say you have retirement assets (a couple of 401(k)s, perhaps) and taxable accounts such as individual, joint, and trust accounts. It takes a coordinated plan to best diversify and allocate your wealth

> **It takes a coordinated plan to best diversify and allocate your wealth across those different investment accounts.**

across those different investment accounts. That means that even if different firms hold those assets, you'll want to work with an advisor on an integrated management plan.

In chapters 4 and 5, we'll cover asset risks and solutions. Families tend to have their guard up when discussing the breadth of their assets, so we focus on communication. As an independent firm, and as a fiduciary, we need to be familiar with the family's overall wealth so that we can recommend financial planning, legal, tax, gifting, insurance, and business options to help you and your family make decisions in your best interest.

III. YOUR LEGACY AT RISK

When it comes to your legacy at risk, every family must be aware of two important pieces. There's the portion of your legacy that ties to your assets and estate—your material wealth. But there is another—and perhaps more important—aspect of your legacy: one that ties to nonmaterial values, such as morals, beliefs, and responsibilities.

When a patriarch and matriarch plan their legacy, they're not just concerned about what happens to their material wealth. They're concerned about what happens to the people, causes, and communities they care for. They're planning so that their material wealth can play a lasting role in continuing to enrich what they love, even long after they're gone.

Avoiding risks to your legacy means more than just having a well-thought-out financial plan for your passing and beyond. We've found the most successful legacies are those passed on with a high degree of transparency and communication from the matriarch and patriarch. When they're open and shared, the next generations can respond favorably and become responsible stewards of the family's wealth.

The biggest obstacle to passing on a legacy, we've seen, is lack of communication regarding both material assets, like real estate, and intangible values.

We're thankful we can facilitate communication by playing a helpful role in educating our clients and the next generation. The ins and outs of investing can be easily misunderstood. Educating a family's growing children and grandchildren to be their own best financial advocates helps us all make better decisions and brings stability and harmony to a family's legacy.

When discussing a plan and legacy with all the people who make up a large, often blended, multigenerational family, the situation has the potential to become stressful or complicated. In our approach, we look to de-stress the situation and strive for simplicity.

Every client has a different comfort level when it comes to providing financial information, and that can change over the course of a lifetime. We've had patriarchs and matriarchs who at first were reluctant to share any financial details with their children and grandchildren. As they learned the importance of transparency and the power of education in preventing risk, they became more accepting of open communication.

Whatever your level of comfort, we believe in the need for communication—even if we only review the overall structure of the family estate, explaining the various entities without referencing monetary figures. From there, we believe in working with your children to build their financial plan. In our firm, we are simultaneously providing those children and grandchildren with an education so that they can be responsible stewards of the family's wealth.

After working with future generations over the years, we've had many patriarchs and matriarchs boast about how proud they are of their children. They've seen their children develop a newfound understanding of the investment world and a sense of responsibility for the family's wealth. Oftentimes, this shared understanding is enough to inspire full communication and encourage prior generations to pull back the curtain.

Lastly, we believe that by sharing this message with you, we can have a positive influence on how our clients and the overall financial industry approach wealth. We believe this message can help achieve greater results for society, creating a more positive and lasting impact on us all for generations to come.

The only remaining question is, how *exactly* do we do this?

OUR INCLUSIVE, FAMILY-FOCUSED APPROACH TO WEALTH

When it comes to your family's finances, making decisions is not easy. The traditional norms often result in a family being forced to make a decision after the death of the primary breadwinner and decision maker. Such unplanned-for decisions may prove to be unnecessarily costly and difficult. That's why it's best to plan ahead—to help avoid decision-making paralysis, which may lead to more devastating effects.

As wealth advisors, JR and I know that poor planning and decision-making can present a huge risk to a family's wealth. But the more we educate families, include all involved parties in financial planning (especially the spouse), and expand the traditional definition of value beyond returns, the better we can protect your wealth from risk. It's your responsibility to play an active role in your and your family's understanding, and it's our responsibility to be your guide.

We wrote this book to be a reader-friendly, instructional guide to our approach to managing a family's wealth and future. In the chapters ahead we will introduce you to the Archer, Bates, Carpenter, and Daniels families. We share their stories of inspiration and tribulations to help you learn from and apply other clients' experiences and perspectives to your own life.

The stories we include should help you understand *why*—why this book and its applied guidance can be so transformative for you.

These families are composites of our clients and their real-life experiences, though we have changed names and identifying characteristics to protect their privacy. We are passionate about these stories because of how relatable they are to us all. Storytelling helps us learn from another's situation, to foresee opportunities for our own family. It's our hope that these stories provide you with a degree of clarity and confidence as to how to navigate your own situation, as well as insight on how to move forward.

The overall arc of the book will take you through the three largest areas of risk to family wealth—estate, assets, and legacy—presenting a set of related subtopics and stories to showcase our family-oriented approach to wealth management.

As for the insight in each chapter—the *how*—we've shared a set of topics and solutions expanding on our approach to helping families with risks. Topics include our recommendations to avoid asset, estate, and legacy risks and how to chart a better wealth plan for you and those you love. Overarching themes that will be covered include communication and dealing with decision-making paralysis, which tend to bridge all three of the main topics.

We wrote *Family Value at Risk* to be a wake-up call to families like yours and for our industry at large. We must start connecting the idea of "value" to family values and envision a more modern, holistic, comprehensive, and integrated version of family wealth planning.

To accomplish our big goals, we believe the financial industry must be more inclusive as a profession. When both men and women advisors collaborate to share their points of view with clients, the overall results can stand the test of time. Such inclusion and equality makes for a more positive experience for those of us who work in the industry, while also contributing to a better client experience. And when families themselves show up equally—including spouses and all related parties—we can account for all family dynamics that affect a household's wealth. Only then can we truly preserve family value from risk.

THE POWER OF DIVERSE PERSPECTIVES: WHY WE NEED MORE WOMEN IN FINANCE

We know the world is evolving rapidly, but in some areas, evidence of that evolution is harder to come by. While women compose nearly 50 percent of financial services employees, they represent a mere 15 percent of industry executives.[2] If our true goal is to help families prosper, that has to change.

Having a diverse range of opinions and perspectives is key to building a full picture when it comes to family wealth. That means we must broaden the conversations to include female family members and advisors alike.

It certainly hasn't been easy for woman to break into the typical "boys' club" of the wealth management industry. This and many other reasons are the causes for the absence of women in the financial field.

Advising is about helping families overcome some of the toughest obstacles in life, celebrate their most meaningful milestones, and provide for their loved ones while they're living and after they are gone. It's about giving people helpful tools that they can use to make the best possible decisions, regardless of what comes their way.

We believe that if more women understood the true goal of the job—or what it could be—they would consider this path, and the industry would begin to benefit from some of the diversity it so desperately needs.

---

2   "Five Things You Need to Know About Women in Finance," *Forbes*, June 5, 2018, https://www.forbes.com/sites/forbesmarketplace/2018/06/05/5-things-you-need-to-know-about-women-in-finance/#694b99014e77.

CHAPTER 1
LESSONS LEARNED

1. **Open communication** between all parties, including spouses, kids, advisors, and other centers of influence

   a. Ensures everyone is on the same page

   b. Helps secure a better overall result

2. **Combat decision-making paralysis**

   a. Take on each task, one step at a time

   b. Build in guard rails and deadlines to keep yourself on track

3. **Keep it simple**

   a. Don't settle for having to sift through fifty pages of material to find your accounts' performance. Request simplicity from your advisor so nothing is lost in translation.

FAMILY ESTATE AT RISK

In chapter 2, JR introduces the Archer family, who over generations has exemplified the family-value approach to estate planning. He explains the big estate risks, such as probate and falling behind in making updates to your plan. He emphasizes how to understand your will, prepare yourself for those estate risks, and get ahead of life events that can derail your family's future. Vanessa, meanwhile, shares a personal story about what drove her to make the decision to start her own estate planning.

Many years ago, we were introduced to an entrepreneurial family, the Archers, at a charity event. The Archers made an immediate, positive impression on us. Shortly after the event, we became their financial advisors. We worked together to expand the focus from just their investment returns to their overall wealth. Over the course of generations, they've proven to be a family that above all prioritizes their harmony.

As we learned in chapter 1, many investors and advisors traditionally apply a limited, exclusionary definition to wealth. Today, we know the power of a broader definition of wealth, one that includes all of a family's estate, assets, and legacy.

The Archers came to model this inclusive definition of wealth. As the decades went by, they became more concerned about family dynamics and responsibly passing on a legacy of wealth stewardship. This has made a huge difference in the family's ability to avoid the risks that sadly have a negative impact on so many other families.

From day one of our advising relationship with the Archer family, we worked with both the elder patriarch and matriarch. They were the original breadwinners and decision makers, and with that in mind, both spouses would come to investment meetings. The Archers in many ways were pioneers of their time with respect to the financial industry, and it was yet another reason why we admired them so much.

The Archers ran a family business, and over the years they spun off some income to diversify into a portfolio with us. Later, we guided them through the sale of their business and managing the liquidity that followed. When they were flush with wealth and a diverse portfolio, we worked diligently with the couple on their estate, assets, and legacy.

After the business windfall, we helped coordinate gifting strategies to fund trust accounts for the children and worked with the couple to proactively educate the next generation on becoming responsible stewards of the family's wealth.

Over the years we have established individual relationships with all five Archer children. Today, we are not only their wealth advisors; we also consider ourselves part of their extended family. In many ways, the Archer family has grown along with our firm. Their approach to wealth has evolved alongside ours, and today we are proud to serve the fourth generation of the family.

Like many who are self-made, the original Archer couple had an early concern with how to give to the next generation in a way that was best for them and their future. They worried that by gifting too aggressively, they might create a situation in which their children and grandchildren wouldn't be as wise with their wealth as they wanted next generations to be and would be forever dependent on the money they had received from prior generations. Such a situation wouldn't be the first or last case in history of subsequent generations imprudently spending the wealth of their forebears.

As their wealth advisors, we had an important role in making sure the wealth remained in good hands—those of our multigenerational team. While our founder, Gene, was nearer to the ages of the patriarch and matriarch, Vanessa and I are closer to that of the children and grandchildren. We've been able to connect to and work well with the younger generations, helping them slowly build their financial literacy.

As the elder Archer couple saw the next generations learn prudence and become capable stewards of their finances, they became more comfortable and more open to gifting to trusts. Once they sold their business, they were able to transfer substantial wealth to the next generations.

Since then, the family has been able to build upon that original wealth. They have allowed it to multiply and flourish. In turn, it has been there to help supplement the income of the next generations. The Archer matriarch and patriarch, our original clients, passed when they were in their nineties, and due in large part to their prudence, the entire Archer family has continued to thrive over the years.

Of course, the family has had its struggles, but its members have been able to maintain the stability of their wealth. Other families haven't managed nearly as well, experiencing financial instability that only compounds their challenges—even turning the challenges into lasting tragedies.

What can we learn from the Archers?

From the beginning, both spouses committed to collaborating on the family's decisions. Later, they expanded that process to include the children. The fact that the patriarch wasn't the sole decision maker for the family's wealth continued to be a big differentiator for them.

While the patriarch passed away a number of years ago, followed by the matriarch soon after, their family continues to live out their wishes in regard to the management and use of their wealth. It was their original commitment to spousal and multigenerational collaboration that greatly contributed to the family's decades of harmony and financial stability.

As Vanessa mentioned in chapter 1, it was once more common for the primary breadwinner to make financial decisions and not share those with the family. Upon the decision maker's passing, such families were often left to sort out a financial mess and forced to make decisions quickly that weren't in their best long-term interest.

We have seen these unfortunate situations play out again and again. Part of the reason for writing this book was to challenge the industry to embrace an approach designed to prevent these risks and prioritize family wealth and harmony.

The Archer family and its many generations make for an excellent example of what a family can achieve when they apply a more inclusive definition to an FVR approach to wealth. It's not always easy, but it's worth it when you see the stability that it can bring to a family's dynamics.

YOUR ESTATE AT RISK

We've grouped this book's guidance into the three main areas of risk: estate, assets, and legacy. In this chapter and the next, we will explore your estate. This may seem counterintuitive; most people think about their assets first when it comes to financial planning. But your estate merits significant consideration up front, because it presents the *largest* risk. If your estate isn't in order, the consequences—tax and otherwise—may potentially offset thirty years of compounding investment returns. That makes it quite pressing.

I came up in the "old world" of advising. Picture the Wall Street broker, the man in the corner office pitching a new offering to his client while smoking a pipe. All that mattered was investment returns. He'd build up as much wealth as he could and then let the attorneys and accountants sort out the rest.

On the surface, results were good. This mentality meant we brought in strong returns for clients, minimized investment risks, and were able to stimulate growth for the overall value of the portfolios. Beneath the surface, however, we began noticing some less-than-ideal trends.

Often, we would work with an investor to accumulate wealth, only to see the family lose a significant portion of it to probate. We'd spend years educating an investor, only to watch the investor pass away, survived by a spouse who found herself starting from square one.

Once you've experienced enough of the risks Vanessa described in chapter 1, you realize how much greater value we can offer clients by taking a holistic approach.

As we've opened our minds to the FVR approach and the decision-making dynamics of both spouses, we've been able to go through a much deeper process. We're now able to discover the wealth and values that clients are trying to pass along—and help them do so successfully.

The merits of high-performing investment portfolios mean little if they don't integrate with the rest of a family's wealth, including next generations. The wealth could get lost to unplanned legal or tax situations. Gaining such understanding has revolutionized our approach.

Serving families with this new approach keeps me passionate day in and day out. I believe that if more firms replicate what we're doing, we would all be better off. We have the opportunity to attain lasting harmony and stability for families. If we are mindful of a family's true value, and overcome today's risk, we'll all enjoy a better tomorrow.

This bright future starts with reverse-engineering your family's wealth, beginning with your estate plan. If we can impart one thing to you as you read this book, it would be to prioritize estate planning. To do that, we'll help you understand three factors:

- Key considerations when crafting a will

- Titling of your assets to avoid probate risk

- Estate taxes with respect to both federal and state thresholds

YOUR WILL

I'm sure you've heard the question many times before: *"Do you have a will?"*

What are people really asking when they pose that question? *When you (and your spouse) die, what happens legally to your wealth and to your dependents?*

Here's one answer: Without a will, the courts decide for you.

Simple enough, but that doesn't make it any easier to address. And I am just as guilty as many of you out there. After having children, I finally brought myself to sit down and create one. Most people avoid creating a will because it can be an emotional, time-consuming process to sort through the messy business of planning for your death. The situation can be especially challenging if you (and your spouse) have a modern family, with a mix of dependents and relatives involved.

Without a will, the courts decide for you.

But do you know what's messier than establishing a will? Burdening your family and the courts with the decisions you didn't make when you could have. We've seen courts decide how a family and its wealth should be handled when there is not a will in place, and it's never the best situation.

What if you don't have a lot of money? If you have children, you still need a will. You cannot just assume that a relative will take care of them. Before they go into a relative's care, a court will adjudicate the decision in lieu of what would have been plainly described in a simple will.

One of our clients, Ben, a third-generation member of the Archer family, was in the process of creating his own will and trust. He was struggling with the same thing that many of us do: sitting down with an attorney to draft it. Ben has two young children, a two-year-old boy and a four-year-old girl. He came into the office recently to discuss his plan. "Ben, where is your will?" I prodded him. "What happens if and when you and your wife pass away? What are you going to do?"

"We already decided—they're going to be taken care of by my wife's brother," he said.

"Okay," I said, "is that in writing?"

Ben shrugged. "My brother-in-law said he's on board. We'll make it official later."

The only "will" he had at the time was a sheet of paper that he and his wife had written up themselves. They had created it a few years before when they were going on a trip and they needed to get something in writing about what should happen with their daughter, just in case. But they had written it quickly and hadn't updated it since. This was particularly problematic, because since they had drafted it, they had a son, who was unaccounted for.

Perhaps the document would stand up in court, but what if it didn't? It is crucial to make sure to draft a will as soon as you begin to grow your family. Include any unborn children, and make sure to update it as you add to your family to avoid any issues regarding their care and inheritance. Doing so may pose an emotional challenge, but getting it done will save your dependents and family undue burden.

It may sound overly enthusiastic for me to push Ben—and you—to have a will. Like Ben, you may be young. And most younger people believe they're *not* going to die anytime soon—myself included. But the truth is that the unthinkable happens every day; we need to be prepared to best protect our family.

Bottom line: a will is a must-have item, especially when you're younger, with dependents who aren't yet adults. If you don't have a will in place, put down the book and take the necessary first steps to drafting a will of your own.

KEEPING YOUR WILL CURRENT

When you're older, a will becomes less of an issue. The trust(s) you have matter more.

When you're thirty or forty years old and have young children, a will should have details about who would take over your children's care—a critical concern. But after they're adults, a will only needs to account for your assets.

At that point, you may find that there are actually fewer details to account for. Your will may essentially become two lines, instructing the reader to move any assets into your trust. Regardless, keeping things current is of the utmost importance.

A friend of mine was recently quite sick. He had always said that he wanted to leave a portion of his life insurance to his mother and the rest to his children. When I asked him if he had updated his plan to reflect his wishes, he said yes. He'd talked to the office plan administrator about it and was sure she'd updated it. On multiple occasions, I told him to make sure, and he assured me he would.

Unfortunately, he passed away at the young age of fifty-nine. Turns out, the updates were never made. What he and many forget is that there are always consequences to not taking the right steps. Thankfully, his kids upheld their father's wishes, and to uphold them, the children decided to give their grandmother the promised gift over a span of ten years, to not exceed the annual exclusion amount.

Yet another benefit of our recommended approach is becoming familiar not only with the terms and details of your will but also with your family. As such, if and when changes need to be made, we can help flag them for your attention and implement them throughout the will and/or trust(s). In life's later stages, your trusts matter more. But a will is always necessary—no matter your age or how much money you have—whether you have $10,000 to your name or billions of dollars in the bank. Everybody needs a will, especially those with children.

Your children's future is more important than any wealth decision you need to plan for. If you haven't created a will, hopefully this is a wake-up call. And if you do have one, hopefully you'll take a moment now to make sure it's current, helping your family avoid additional and unnecessary pain.

VANESSA'S TAKE:
THE AIRPLANE NIGHTMARE

Full disclosure: despite having a current will and trust, I personally encountered a situation that taught me an important lesson.

We were headed off on a family vacation to Mexico. It was not until the airplane took off and we had horrible turbulence that I held my kids and began to pray. Then I looked around at my various family members on the plane and suddenly wondered, *What happens if we crash and everyone dies?*

Seated with me on the plane were my mother, my father, my cousin and her daughter, my two sisters, their husbands, their children, and my children—basically anyone I was planning to leave something to was on this airplane!

I'm a little embarrassed to share this story, but I do so because it was a big learning experience for me. For one, I realized we should never have my entire family on one airplane. I know that sounds like common sense, but you may not think about it when you're booking a trip. However, the bigger realization for me was that I had to reevaluate my plan and make sure it held up to all situations.

When I returned home, I reviewed my will and trust. I had both my Plan A and Plan B recipients accounted for. But then I decided to take it one step further and added a Plan C, a beloved nonfamily member who's unlikely to travel with the family.

I learned from the trip that while having a Plan B might seem like enough, it is important to always have a Plan C.

Plan C is necessary. I know that it's horrible to sit there with the attorney and go through all the questions. "Okay, then if your sister dies, then what?"

"Then I have my other sister."

"Well what if your other sister dies?"

It's easy to feel as if that attorney is wiping out your whole family with her words. But the reality is that in this instance, that could've happened on the plane. And that makes Plan C essential. Don't set it and forget it! Reconsider, reevaluate, and make those adjustments.

THE PROBATE RISK TO YOUR ESTATE: HOW TO AVOID SURPRISES

Let's talk about probate—the judicial process of authenticating a will and distributing your estate. Are your checking and savings accounts in title of your trust or in joint tenants? A bank account in your name is just one example of an asset that may potentially be subject to probate upon your death. Whatever assets you have that remain in your individual name, besides retirement accounts (i.e., IRAs, 401(k) s, etc.), may face probate.

The value of your estate can also trigger probate. Even carefully planned estates can require probate if the value of assets passing under the will exceeds the maximum amount that your state allows to be transferred under a small estates affidavit[3]. In Illinois specifically, if you have any amount over $100,000 in your individual name, it's subject to probate court. For example, if you have $600,000 in your individual name, that full amount is subject to probate, whereas if you

---

3    $100,000 in Illinois, for example.

have $99,999, you can transfer based on your will without having to go through the probate court process.

Many clients typically focus only on their real estate and financial assets. However, all assets passing under your will need to be considered. Assets owned in your individual name will pass based on the stipulations of your will. Common assets that clients forget to consider when determining if they are over the maximum allowable amount include furniture, jewelry, and cars, as well as property owned as tenants-in-common.

Many wills now allow the testator—or person drafting the will—to leave a memorandum stating who should receive certain items of furniture, jewelry, and art that the deceased accumulated over the course of her lifetime. What happens if you don't do this? We can look to two recent client cases to find out.

While visiting a recently deceased client's family, an attorney was handed a memorandum written by the deceased listing certain items of personal property and stating whom the client wanted to receive each listed item. Many of the items were quite valuable. These items alone would have required the estate to be probated.

Families don't often think about this. Rather, they merely pass these items to the intended recipients after the owner dies and never consider that they may have to be included in the probate estate because ownership is usually determined by possession, not by a registered title, like a car or boat has. The lawyer was now in an awkward position. She could not ethically prepare an affidavit, which needs to be signed under penalties of perjury, without listing these assets.

This problem could have been avoided if the client had signed an assignment of personal property, transferring all property that does not have a registered title into the client's trust. It was too late for that simple fix because the client was already deceased.

Another lawyer went to visit a dying client at his home to say goodbye and ensure the client's affairs were in order. The door to the garage was open when the lawyer pulled into the driveway. The lawyer noticed two relatively new cars in the garage! Upon investigation, it was determined that both cars were titled in the name of the dying client. Luckily, the lawyer had sufficient time to run to the DMV and have the titles transferred into the client's wife's name. Otherwise, the value of those cars would have pushed the client's probate assets above the small estate limit.

The distinction about trusts—most typically a revocable living trust—is that you must fund them during your lifetime. That is, to avoid probate, your liquid and invested assets should be held in your trust and/or titled in your trust's name. Be careful, we have seen investors assume that once you establish a trust, your assets are automatically titled in the trust name. That is not true; you need to physically move the assets over into the trust and/or retitle assets into it.

Imagine if you passed tomorrow—all those great investment returns may not benefit your family in the manner you intended, considering the amount that could be forfeited in probate. Why take the risk?

What should you do right now to help protect your assets for future generations? If you have a living revocable trust, be certain to assign ownership of all untitled tangible personal property to the trust while you are able! Also, make sure you know how every piece of property you own is titled to ensure it will not be included in your probate estate.

YOUR STATE'S PROBATE THRESHOLD AND ESTATE TAXES

As I mentioned earlier, the probate threshold for Illinois is $100,000, as of 2019. That amount is specific to Illinois. Every state is different, so make sure to check your state to see what your applicable threshold is.

I emphasize your state's tax and probate laws because most families only think about the federal law and not their state as well. You may have additional risk to bear if you don't account for your state's unique probate threshold estate tax.

As of 2019, the Illinois estate tax threshold is $4 million. This means a family doesn't need to have upwards of $20 million to plan for their estate. If you live in Illinois and your estate is worth more than $4 million, it may be at risk.

When estate planning with our families, we help them through the nuances of probate, trusts, and individual accounts. By understanding all their assets and titling, we can not only avoid probate but often minimize or prevent any unnecessary estate tax.

BOTTOM LINE: PREPARE YOURSELF TO MANAGE YOUR ESTATE PLAN

We've explained how you benefit from prioritizing your will and understanding the risks presented by probate and taxes. In chapter 3, we'll get into more detail, fully explaining our FVR approach to trusts and a multigenerational estate plan.

Estate planning requires you to prepare your heirs, but before you can do that, you have to first prepare yourself.

NET WORTH STATEMENT

The net worth statement, we believe, is the most important tool in understanding and coordinating your assets. This is the tool we start with when planning for your estate.

The net worth statement is a one-page overview of your assets and liabilities, so we can track titling and values. This financial statement will include your insurance, investments, real estate, and more.

Our one-page net worth statement is a snapshot of a family's most essential information to help avoid as many risks as possible. Behind the scenes, we delve into the details and carefully analyze what the whole picture looks like. But we strive for simplicity and transparency to help ensure that families understand their estate and avoid any unnecessary burdens.

In chapter 5, we'll dive further into the net worth statement. At the end of that chapter, we've also included a tear-off sheet with a sample net worth statement so you can see the full picture of how a net worth statement can benefit you.

Along with a will, everybody should have a net worth statement. With these two documents as your baseline, we can develop the multigenerational estate plan that best suits your family's values today and tomorrow and for future generations.

While our approach starts with the simple goal of including everyone involved, the mechanics that make the goal attainable are as complex as the family and its associated estate. Our success is in helping a family understand and sort through the complexity, to make the best decisions for their lasting stability.

The Archers prioritized an FVR approach to their estate, assets, and legacy. They had great ideas that we learned from; they also followed many of our recommendations and did what was best for their family.

CHAPTER 2
LESSONS LEARNED

- While estate, assets, and legacy risks can represent long-term threats to your overall wealth, a lack of communication is the biggest contributor to the loss of family wealth and value.

- We can't stress enough that everyone, yes, everyone needs a will. You can eliminate the risk of the court deciding guardianship for your minor children by creating and maintaining a will.

- Establishing a trust can be vital to ensure your assets and value are protected and directed as you desire. But for your trust to be effective, it must be "funded." What do we mean by that? Your assets should be titled in the name of the trust. Be sure to check on key assets such as homes, cars, bank accounts, artwork, and jewelry to make certain that these assets are covered by your trust directives.

CHAPTER 3

DEVELOPING A MULTIGENERATIONAL ESTATE PLAN

In chapter 3, Vanessa tells the story of the Carpenter family, who almost faced a disastrous disinheritance mess. She explains the multigenerational estate plan, which involves spouses, children, and grandchildren to prepare the entire family for a harmonious and secure future.

Trusts are key, and Vanessa covers the ins and outs of how to use them to help families transfer wealth from one generation to the next. Lastly, Vanessa helps prepare you and your family for the life events you'll experience, noting when to review and update your plan.

The story of the Archer family, which opened chapter 2, is unfortunately the exception, not the rule. More often, families take a less inclusive approach to their finances. As you know by now, that exclusivity can compound problems as the years go by.

The more common situation is that of the Carpenter family, whose patriarch began working with us years ago, and who, like the Archers, have continued to collaborate with us for four generations. But in the Carpenters' case, the patriarch never agreed to take an inclusive approach to the family wealth. He kept his finances close to the vest. He did not communicate any finance-related details to his spouse or children.

In his original trust, written decades ago when his grandchildren were very young or yet to be born, he stipulated that they could not marry someone outside the family's faith if they were to inherit his wealth. Despite this clearly delineated term in the trust, some of the grandchildren didn't seem to get the memo. Over the years, they married people of other faiths.

As he entered his nineties, the patriarch's health declined, but the terms of the trust remained the same. We—along with other members of the family—began to worry there would be issues when passing wealth to his grandchildren. This was a huge risk and would likely cause family strife.

The purpose of a trust is to keep a set of rules in place. We must follow it to the letter of the law. With that in mind, the last thing we want would be for just *one* grandchild to actually marry a person of the same faith and thus be the only one eligible to inherit. That could start an argument between the grandchildren.

However, avoiding all that risk and stress would require a very simple adjustment: the patriarch could amend the trust.

With our dynamic pairing of a female and male advisor, we were able to have a meeting with the Carpenter patriarch to express our concern with the current terms of the trust. He had decided on the terms long ago—did he now want to amend them?

When he had first created the trust, half a lifetime earlier, the world was very different. Society wasn't as open as it is today. And the grandchildren were babies. But we didn't know if the Carpenter patriarch had changed in his thinking as time went on. Neither did he, until we brought up the subject.

We discussed how the grandchildren had grown up and had built families of their own. He had seen the happiness they had cultivated with their respective spouses, despite their different faiths.

After we expressed our concern, he paused our conversation for a moment. He seemed surprised—not by the fact that we had raised this particular conversation but by his mindset from years past. Fortunately, with time, the corresponding changes in society, and the opportunity to get to know the spouses of his grandchildren, he realized the weight of his prior decision. This also made him understand what he needed to do to achieve the impact he wanted after he was gone.

With the holistic, inclusive approach that we take as advisors, we help families avoid or at least understand catastrophic consequences. Such terms in a trust would cause a multigenerational rift in the family's wealth and harmony. We work to get ahead of such risks, so that when the primary breadwinner and decision maker passes away, they're able to establish multigenerational stability.

We believe the most harmonious, stable option is to embrace an FVR approach to your estate and trusts. Once the end of life comes, you can be sure everything is in place. You can be sure of your family's future even when you're gone.

Many families are like the Carpenters. They put off decisions for years, misguidedly thinking that the consequences don't apply to them. In reality, we've seen that there are consequences, and they have an impact on families of every walk of life. No one is exempt.

Here's an example from another family we are working with.

As we write this, the patriarch is gravely ill and in the hospital. The family's estate plan has remained disorganized for several years, ever since his wife passed away, in fact. There are documents waiting for his signature.

If he passes away during this current hospital stay, without signing the documents and retitling the assets into the trust's name, his estate will go to probate court. If that happens, the court will likely tax his holdings to the tune of about $1 million. For his three children, this huge tax burden would be devastating to their stability.

We share the story of the Carpenters—and others like it—to show how a family's approach to wealth can evolve over the years. Starting with a traditional view, the patriarch and family eventually confronted the need to embrace inclusivity. This would mean amending their trusts as part of creating a multigenerational estate plan, which is the subject of this chapter. In the following pages, we'll show you how this evolves.

HOW TO AVOID RISKS WITH A MULTIGENERATIONAL ESTATE PLAN

Like the Carpenters, many families have estate plans that at first glance seem fine, but upon closer inspection contain underlying risks.

Often, a family may have unsigned documents, new family members, marriages, divorces, and health crises both physical and mental and may experience any number of situations or life events that can present risks to an estate plan's intentions. Our approach helps families stay on top of those changes, so that they don't find themselves with outdated documents that could result in an unintentional disaster.

We attribute a large part of our harmonious and stable estate planning to our female-male advisor dynamic. Rarely is it the male clients who share with us the family dynamics we need to truly understand to make our best recommendations. More often, it's the women—the mothers, female family members, and female advisors—who help us understand and navigate these issues. As a female advisor, I can easily relate to the women in the room, often anticipating their questions (because they are the ones I would have asked myself).

> **We attribute a large part of our harmonious and stable estate planning to our female-male advisor dynamic.**

By being present for these discussions, the little moments and big milestones that make up a family's life, and tackling the advising work that must occur in between, we're able to offer the best advice possible. We're there for our clients, helping celebrate a newborn or sort out the difficult details that accompany one's passing. We've cried at weddings and funerals alike and brought balloons or treats for many birthdays. Even though we are not able to attend all our clients' life events, we are there for them, both mentally and emotionally.

Getting to know a family over generations helps us to avoid risks that occur naturally throughout their lives. In executing a family's intentions, our approach is based on developing a *multigenerational estate plan*, which we review every time they have a major life event.

Ahead, we'll define the multigenerational estate plan and expand on how trusts can be the best vehicle to transfer wealth. We'll explore the life events that require a review or update to keep your plan current and close with a case for financial advisorship that integrates your estate planning.

WHAT IS A MULTIGENERATIONAL ESTATE PLAN?

A multigenerational estate plan is one that spans the lives of the matriarch, the patriarch, and their heirs. That doesn't mean that there has to be one cohesive plan; it just means that whatever estate planning you do should coordinate with the plans of the next generation. The mistake many families make is assuming the plan is complete once they merely account for the next generation. However, an estate plan that is truly multigenerational is not complete until the heirs' estate plans are then re-coordinated with the matriarch and patriarch's, so that everything aligns. If we could divide this process into two parts, they would be as follows:

- Understanding the next generation's financial situation, both presently and what it may be like in the future

- Reviewing current laws and analyzing what steps can be taken to optimize both taxes and gifting

Why is this approach advantageous?

Once these two steps are taken, we are able to see why this approach is so beneficial. We saw in the Archer family how the transparency between generations allowed gifting to benefit both the giver and receiver. Since there was full disclosure between generations, both parties could see why, in some cases, it would be beneficial to skip a generation—thus allowing those individuals to save on taxes that could otherwise wipe out the value of the gift.

Coordination and continuous review enabled everyone to ensure their plans addressed individual and family needs, regardless of the situations that arose. For example, if there was a divorce in the next generation, the matriarch and patriarch could re-coordinate and adjust the estate plan, making sure that the ex-spouse would not have an inheritance. Or it could ensure that families who experience a windfall before they are set to inherit won't risk losing money if receiving a planned inheritance would push them into another tax bracket—thus negating the value of the gift. Instead, the matriarch and patriarch can earmark the gift for their grandchildren. Everyone can simply adjust and distribute the family wealth in a different manner.

WHY A TRUST?

Many people perceive trusts as complex vehicles that only ultra-wealthy families use. Trusts can be an extremely valuable tool for managing money, both during your life and after you're gone. When estate planning with families, we present a high-level overview of their trust options to find what's best for them. There are volumes of books on the intricacies of trusts. Our purpose here is to share some benefits our families find most compelling. A trust allows you to

- keep the money in the family and protected from creditors,

- set terms to be followed after your passing, and

- review and update your wishes.

Let's break these benefits down a bit further.

I. KEEP THE MONEY IN THE FAMILY

Trusts can keep the money in the family, regardless of what "family" means to you. Remember: family isn't just bloodline, as we so frequently see today.

There are many modern families now that are defined by more than genetics. Having a blended family myself, I know the importance of stating our connections. It can be frustrating or sad that we have to stipulate this legally, but it's essential for me and others who are planning to pass wealth on to those who aren't bound to us by blood.

On the other hand, some may make the decision to not pass on wealth to a descendant for a variety of reasons. For example, we work with a patriarch and matriarch who have two children: one who has an extraordinarily successful business and another who, despite being a hardworking director of a nonprofit, is a low-income single parent of three. The patriarch and matriarch took an approach that was fair, but not equal, when it came to distributing their assets. They determined that the wealthy child would inherit some property but no other assets, while the other sibling and grandchildren would be provided for.

Regardless of who receives the inheritance, the terms are up to you to decide as the matriarch and patriarch. You have innumerable options and avenues to do what's best for you and your family's future. And you have the flexibility to change these fair but not equal decisions at any time.

FAIR VS. EQUAL: NAVIGATING TOUGH CONVERSATIONS

While you're in control when it comes to how to distribute your wealth and determining whether it's more important to keep things fair or equal, making those decisions isn't always easy—or well received.

Not long ago I was on a flight and working on this book. The friendly woman next to me glanced over at my laptop screen and asked me what I was doing, and we began chatting about this project and our message. Then, she opened up, sharing her story—and the pain of navigating a difficult conversation regarding her inheritance—with me.

One day, her father called her into his office. "Honey," he

said, "I need to talk to you about something."

"Sure," she replied. "What is it, Dad?"

"Well, you and your husband have done so well for your-selves. Meanwhile, your brothers and sisters are struggling. They need help a lot more than you do. So, I've decided to leave all my assets to them."

The woman was taken aback. She began to cry. It wasn't about the money itself; it was about feeling connected to her family. She felt as if, with his decision, her father was telling her she wasn't part of the family anymore. She didn't want things to be equal, per se, but she did want them to be fair—at least in terms of recognizing that she had a place in his plans.

There are many ways to make your heirs feel as if they are a part of the plan, without providing them with an equal distribution of your estate. For example, you can decide to make them a part of the family foundation, enabling them to carry on the charitable legacy of the family. You can bequeath real estate property or heirlooms, rather than funds. All these options allow those closest to you to feel that they made an impact on your life.

Communication can also make a tremendous difference. When you explain the rationale behind your decisions, you provide your loved ones with the opportunity to understand where you're coming from and to express their feelings about the decision.

That actually made all the difference for the woman I met on the plane. When she told her father about how she felt, he decided to adjust his plan, giving her a portion of his estate.

> Later on, when her father held a formal family meeting, for which all the siblings flew in to discuss his plans, she was part of that conversation, which ended up meaning a great deal to them both.
>
> What's the moral of this story? Don't be afraid to divide things fairly rather than equally, but remember that communication is of the utmost importance. Do it early and often to make sure everyone is on the same page and avoid hurt feelings.

II. SET TERMS

Once you decide to whom the wealth should transfer, you can set terms to ensure it is used responsibly. For example, you can add specific terms to the trust that restrict when beneficiaries have access to the funds, how much they can use at a time, and what the funds can be used for.

Time and again, we've seen first-generation patriarchs and matriarchs look at their children and grandchildren with apprehension. They worry about what their heirs will do with the legacy they have built. Terms allow you to get your children and grandchildren up to speed. For the vast majority of families we've worked with, the initial apprehension melts away as the years go by and the patriarchs and/or matriarchs see how the next generations responsibly care for the family's wealth.

III. REVIEW AND UPDATE

As with the Carpenters, many families encounter the need to amend or update a trust due to any number of life events. Conveniently, most trusts can be amended without much hassle as new life events—like birth, death, marriage, divorce, and disability—occur.

Too often, life events pass by, and the trust's original intentions become outdated. Make a point to continuously review and update your trust, or commit to working with an advisor who can help remind you of and execute your wishes. That way, your family never has to worry that its best intentions won't be fulfilled based on an outdated document.

Trusts are important components of a multigenerational estate plan, but they should always play into your family's big picture. Having a wealth advisor who is familiar with your estate plan and assets reduces the time it takes to make these updates. Without a comprehensive estate plan that accounts for all your wishes and keeps your documents in order, amending or updating a trust could present a huge challenge.

IS IT TIME TO REVIEW YOUR PLAN?

Families change. It's a reality we've seen play out in countless ways over the decades. As generations unfold, priorities evolve, needs shift, family members come and go. A multigenerational estate plan is only successful if it adapts to your evolving intentions and changing family.

Life events—such as death, birth, marriage, and divorce, to name a handful—can put your estate plan at risk if it isn't reviewed and potentially amended. This means at minimum you should review your estate plan at least every three to five years and, better yet, as major life events occur. Our best recommendation would be to review it every time you have a life event or when estate laws change.

How do you know when it's time to review? If you answer "yes" to any of these questions, your plans merit another look:

- Did you just get married?

- Did you just have another grandchild?

- Are you or any of your beneficiaries recently divorced?

- Did your successor trustee pass away, or was it a bank that no longer exists?

- Have any of your named beneficiaries changed?

- Has your level of wealth dramatically increased or decreased since the plan was last reviewed?

- Are you likely to be the benefactor of an inheritance that you just became aware of?

Looking at the list of questions above, did any of the questions surprise you with respect to their potential to have an impact on your plan? Many of us realize the birth of a new child alters overall distributions, but we may not be aware that the passing of a successor trustee puts at risk the trust and its intentions.

For example, let's say you listed your brother as successor trustee. If he was not able to act due to death or disability, the responsibility would fall on a trust company. This default provision is easily overlooked; if your brother passed away three years ago, you face a significant concern, whether you realize it or not.

Remember my airplane nightmare in chapter 2, in which my whole family was on the same flight and I realized I didn't have a Plan C in place in case the plane went down? We've seen families devastated overnight by such accidents, without a Plan C in place.

A sad passing could befall a beneficiary as well. Such a life event would also require updating one's trust. For example, say your trust details that 20 percent passes to each of five grandchildren. If one passes away, the money could be split among the remaining four. However, many people would prefer that the heirs of the grandchild that passed away inherit their 20 percent. That could only be confirmed if the trust was reviewed and updated after the grandchild passed away.

We hope the previous three points and this discussion of life events gives you the confidence to explore what's best for your family—and to take action.

We all need to be mindful of the options afforded us by a current multigenerational estate plan. Knowing our options helps us have positive wealth advising conversations.

REVIEW YOUR PLAN: THE KEY TO MULTIGENERATIONAL ESTATE PLANNING

The day you create your estate plan, you feel wonderful. With that big task off your to-do list, the temptation is to put it in a drawer and forget about it. But the moment you walk out the door of your attorney's office, life events happen. Your assets and circumstances fluctuate.

> **The key to a multigenerational estate plan is to stay on top of it.**

The key to a multigenerational estate plan is to stay on top of it. Life events should trigger review of your plan much more frequently than you might have thought or done in the past. The importance of having an up-to-date plan increases as life goes on.

How do you account for these changes when your estate plan isn't always top of mind? Go ahead and schedule a review every three to five years. By the same token, you should coordinate with your heirs to make your plans align with theirs.

We emphasize the importance of working with a comprehensive wealth advisor who is aware of your multigenerational dynamics and can help you stay on top of your plan and review it as well. Such an advisor will also stay abreast of the conversations you need to have and the decisions you need to make.

Of course, you're up against a tough adversary: your own mindset. Life events present complex situations and bring to light family dynamics that many want to avoid, leading them into decision-making paralysis—whether the circumstances are positive or negative. The need to review and amend your estate plan because a new grandchild was born. Or perhaps one of your children recently got divorced. Just the thought of it can be overwhelming. A wealth advisor can help you avoid the paralysis inherent in making decisions about your estate and eventual passing.

The best advisors know how to address your complex situations with the most prudent—and typically simplest—solutions possible. But keep in mind that those simple solutions exist only if you and your wealth advisor have done the due diligence necessary to prepare a comprehensive financial and legacy plan in addition to that estate plan.

It's yet another reason why a wealth advisor can make a real difference in your financial future—and that of your children and grandchildren. Without one, you may never make the decisions necessary to achieve your goals. Do the life events I've experienced require a new trust or just amendments? Do I need a brand-new estate plan? What happens now? What happens in a few years when things change yet again? How many hours do I have to sit with my attorney? How much is this going to cost me?

With our FVR approach, reviewing and updating estate plans is just part of our advising process. We wouldn't do it any other way.

So, when life events happen, I can tell you with confidence that you don't have to worry. Since our whole plan is in sync, making the appropriate change typically only requires a one-page amendment. A simple one-pager and those worries disappear.

We'll close this chapter by sharing what happened to the Carpenters. Remember the story that opened this chapter, of the patriarch who put off amending his trust terms so that he could legally transfer wealth to all his grandchildren?

After discussing with him his family dynamics and future under his current, outdated plan, we helped him get in touch with his softer side. We could see he had been experiencing decision-making paralysis. He caused his family years of uncertainty and worry. We acknowledged his feelings and explained that when he eventually passed away, the family would experience years of discord and discontent if the original trust's restrictive terms were to be in place.

So, what happened?

Thankfully, he agreed to amend the terms.

The make-or-break decision—the big, multigenerational risk—was solved with a simple one-page document. With everything else prepared, that's all it took to rescue this family from traumatic generational instability. Just one sheet of paper could mitigate future family angst.

We sat with the Carpenter patriarch as he met with his attorney and amended the terms to include all his grandchildren, regardless of with whom they were partnered. We typed it up in minutes, and after years of putting it off, he signed it and was done. Imagine the relief he must have felt the moment we hit "print."

One of the main takeaways is that it is imperative to review your estate from the top down but then also coordinate with your heirs from the bottom up, to make sure everyone's plans flow together.

If you haven't done so, and your affairs still aren't in order, then any life event will present a mess to sort through. Start planning now, review often—and your wealth won't get in the way of your family's harmony. It will become part of the positive legacy you leave for generations.

CHAPTER 3 TEAR-OFF SHEET

Steps to take when reviewing or creating an estate:

- Have an **estate plan** in place, i.e., will, trust, and powers of attorney for health care and property.

- If you have a living (revocable) trust, be certain it is properly funded.

- **Balance assets** among spouses to reduce potential estate taxes.

- Be certain assets are **properly titled** to avoid probate.

- **Review beneficiary designations** of insurance and qualified plans on an annual basis to be certain they are consistent with your estate plan.

- Review fiduciary (trustee and executor) and guardian appointments on an annual basis.

- Be certain to account for **variances** in state estate tax exemptions and the federal exemption.

- **Coordinate withdrawal rights** and distributions to heirs under your plan to be certain any variances are consistent with your goals.

- Be certain college students over eighteen have a power of attorney for health care.

- Business owners, have a **succession plan** in place to protect the value of your business in the event of your death.

CHAPTER 4

FAMILY ASSETS AT RISK

In chapter 4, JR tells the story of the Bates family, whose members learned that separating one's emotions from one's investments is essential when making investment decisions for a family's future. JR describes how a lack of coordination—while common in traditional investing—often puts our assets at serious risk. By the same token, he explains how engaging in a concentrated effort to arrive on the same page helps families to minimize risk and maximize value.

While many of our client relationships have begun with the matriarch and patriarch, in this case we connected with the Bates children first. The Bates patriarch was a savvy attorney who was able to build a large nest egg through flexible compensation structures. As an attorney, he considered his assets and estate to be under control. He had a financial plan and knew he would leave his family a substantial amount of wealth once he passed.

The problem was, he didn't share this financial plan with his children. Excluded from the estate planning process, they were unaware of all the assets that would transfer to them after his passing.

One of those assets had the potential to cause a great deal of confusion. The Bates patriarch, at the outset of his career, did legal work for a company that could not afford his retainer and fees. So, they agreed to pay him in company stock. As the years went by, he continued to work for this company in exchange for stock, which eventually became a large part of his estate.

As his career went on, the private company continued to grow and distribute income. However, because it was private, he didn't know the company's marketable value, and thus he was unsure of how large the overall value of the stock had become. Holding this stock also posed a liquidity issue, as he was a minority owner in a private company, so he couldn't openly trade his stock. Because he didn't expect to pass away at a young age, he had never discussed this concentrated stock position with his kids or shared why it had grown to the size that it had become.

When he passed away, his children inherited his assets. But because he had never shared with them his intentions, they didn't know what to do with the company stock. Was it an investment he believed in, one that he felt the children should hold on to indefinitely?

A few years later, the private company went public. It was at this point that the Bates daughter sought us out and briefed us on the family history and background. After we reviewed the documentation, we could see that this was a large portion of her estate. We noted that this stock was significantly overweighted in her portfolio and were working on strategies to slowly decrease the size of the position, since the company was now publicly trading. The children looked again at the company and considered the fact that it was not in a growth industry. They discussed whether to keep it or not, but they couldn't come to a consensus.

The daughter decided to sell and diversify, selling her stock at about $80 per share. Meanwhile, the son decided to hold the position. He believed that it was his father's wish, and he wanted to make sure to honor it. The sister recommended on many occasions that her brother should sell, but he didn't listen. When he finally did, it was at just $10 per share. The decisions they each made—to buy and to hold respectively—created a large wealth disparity between the brother and sister, as well as an emotional divide in the family.

When someone passes away, there are always emotions to sort out. Some family members hold on to memories; others hold on to physical items—including assets that their family members previously owned. We've seen time and again that separating yourself from what you think might be an emotional connection to an asset can be a critical step for the family. This is especially true in cases where there has been no clear guidance as to why and how your loved ones came to hold it.

Why do I share this story about family dynamics and emotional investing to begin a chapter covering assets? Your emotions can be one of the largest hurdles to overcome when learning how to invest.

Traditionally, most investors think of investment risk as volatility in the marketplace, meaning that a downturn in the stock market could sink the value of your investments. However, we all see the market's overall long-term trend is to rise. When advisors tell you to sit tight, it's because they know the market will rebound eventually. The risk isn't just in the volatility inherent in the marketplace; it's also in how investors respond to that volatility.

After working with generations of families, we've seen how the *decisions* one makes can affect the family's wealth to a much higher degree than any traditional volatility risks.

Let's say you accumulate assets, such as a portfolio of investments, and they're paying you an income stream of dividends and interest every year. If these assets are mismanaged, you can lose the wealth you have so patiently accumulated.

For instance, if you can't bear the thought of seeing your investments fall during a downturn, you sell out at the bottom. You have now just locked in a loss and will miss out on a potential rebound. Whether it is the COVID-19 crash or the Great Recession of 2008, challenging times will cause these emotional reactions.

VANESSA'S TAKE: THE RISKS OF EMOTIONAL INVESTING

Much like the Bates, many families struggle with the emotional side of investing. It's completely normal to have an emotional knee-jerk response to a situation and want to act on it, thus altering your plans. The trouble is, we've seen that by taking such actions, many families experience the opposite of the intended effect. Their actions cause further strife, rather than avoiding it.

Wealth advisors help you understand your overall situation to avoid the risks of emotional investing. In the heat of the moment—when emotions are reaching their peak— advisors can offer perspective. Your advisor can help you ride out this storm, so you don't make an emotional decision and derail all your hard work.

If you have your coordinated portfolio, and it's generating the income you need, you should be diversified enough to handle any ups and downs in the short term.

Typically, we recommend that families adjust their portfolios to make them more conservative overall during downturns, rather than pull out of the market entirely. But when you see your accounts drop in value, it can be tempting to get out.

We've encouraged so many families not to sell out at the bottom. Doing so can bring significant consequences. The earning power of your wealth may be diminished due to the poor timing of this decision. Without an opportunity to rebound, those losses can be permanent. If you are in retirement, you may have to return to work, and if you are currently working, you could have to work longer or cut down your spending dramatically to meet your goals—or even just stay above water. All that can be hard to see on your own when emotions are clouding your judgment.

Throughout the rest of this chapter, we'll help you better understand your assets, the risks that exist and why they are there, why the 60/40 split is likely outdated, and how coordination alone can help families preserve value.

YOUR ASSETS AT RISK

When your assets are coordinated as part of a comprehensive financial plan, they can help a family enhance the value of their wealth. When *uncoordinated*, assets can pose real risks to that wealth.

In our approach, we account for the many risks out there by helping families develop a comprehensive wealth plan. We coordinate the assets so that they are seldom affected by the common risks to which so many families are subjected.

An uncoordinated plan can present a handful of avoidable risks, including:

- duplicated assets and missed opportunities and

- tax burdens from unplanned liquidity events.

When we begin working with new clients, some have their guard up—particularly during our initial conversations. At first, many are hesitant to discuss their assets beyond the portion they wish to invest with us. This is understandable, considering the industry norm is to want to collect more fees by transferring any outside holdings under management.

However, our coordinated approach comes from a different place. The reason it's helpful for us to be aware of every asset is that knowing *how* those are invested and titled allows us to create a net worth statement. By knowing how, we can build an integrated strategy around our holdings and any outside holdings, creating a comprehensive plan. Through coordination, we are able to avoid duplicating what is already in place or missing an opportunity, thus ensuring the family is properly diversified for the long run.

We also often find that assets are not titled properly, posing many of the risks you've already seen. When we're able to view the outside holdings, we can advise on how to retitle them to help avoid unnecessary losses.

We start working with families at all different phases of life and wealth management, so we ask a variety of questions to help uncover assets, including those they forgot they even had.

Typically, our clients have some or all of the following types of assets:

- stocks
- bonds
- cash and equivalents
- ETFs (exchange-traded funds)
- alternative investments
- insurance products
- real estate
- private equity
- mutual funds
- art and other valuables

By coordinating outside assets, advising on how they're titled, and avoiding these risks, we can get past the industry norm of focusing merely on investments and create a truly comprehensive FVR plan. This approach also shows the value we can add over time.

With that in mind, let's look at an example of the typical, uncoordinated approach to investing.

With many new clients, we find their assets are spread across different accounts and holdings. It's common for a client to have an account at Merrill Lynch and another at Wells Fargo and split their wealth between the two. The split isn't based on performance; it's just a way that clients feel they are diversifying.

Now, within both of these accounts, they spread the wealth between a handful of commonly held assets. Let's say the Merrill Lynch account invests in ETFs and mutual funds, while their account at Wells Fargo invests with different mutual funds.

If we analyze what the two are doing, we will likely find significant overlap—or that they are almost totally redundant. It could be two accounts with two separate firms, but both are invested in a similar index, delivering similar returns, and posing similar risks. Redundancy can cause a duplication of fees, lack of economies of scale, and many inefficiencies that aren't accounted for. Bottom line: an overall lack of planning is common and can be remedied with a coordinated, comprehensive plan.

UNDERSTANDING YOUR RISKS: TWO COMMON SCENARIOS

As you can imagine, because the financial industry is so complex, the details of accounts, their holdings, and the differences between firms can get complicated. Clients usually don't understand the risks of no coordination until they see the benefits of an FVR approach.

Let's look at two risk scenarios. The first risk arises from a client's response to volatility.

Recently, a client called us, asking to sell a portion of his investments. He was worried about the market, and he wanted to be a little more conservative. After discussing his situation and concerns, I reviewed his portfolio. I considered his request as it related to his overall plan, accounting for all his assets, and realized that the growth we'd achieved for him would trigger a large capital gains tax if I sold.

I knew he had accounts with another advisor as well, so I called the advisor to ask about his gains. The client had ETFs and mutual funds with that advisor, which happened to have less unrealized gain compared to our positions. Thus, if those were liquidated, they would not trigger as large a tax burden. We determined that it would be better for the client to sell the holdings he had with his other advisor rather than with us. Then we reworked the overall strategy to make it more conservative, in accordance with his new risk tolerance.

Most financial advisors don't have access to their clients' full financial pictures, which means they may process this client request from a siloed view and blindly trigger unnecessary consequences in the process.

Proper coordination of all assets preserves the value of the wealth you have and avoids the risks, such as a large capital gains burden. Imagine how disappointed the client would have been to see a 12 percent gain in returns throughout the year but see, too, that his return was ultimately lower due to an uncoordinated liquidity event that caused higher taxes!

The second scenario we'll look at shines a light on the potential issues that present themselves in the different ways advisors can interpret your risk tolerance.

Let's say you have assets held at JP Morgan, Merrill Lynch, and Wells Fargo. When you meet with your advisors, you tell them, "This is the level of risk I'm comfortable with." Each advisor then interprets your risk tolerance in a slightly different manner.

Your JP Morgan advisor might say, "Okay, I'm going to give you a 70/30 split based on our discussion." Your Merrill Lynch advisor might say, "I think you're 50/50." And your Wells Fargo advisor says, "No, I think you're 60/40."

When we coordinate your assets in our comprehensive plan, we also coordinate with any and all advisors responsible for your outside holdings. We'll work with them to review your statements. By analyzing your assets across all custodians, we can help evaluate your overall risk.

Accounting for all the holdings, let's say the true level of risk across the board is 70/30. That might be too conservative for you. If that's the case, we're able to rework the assets to bring the ratio more in line with your risk tolerance.

Clients want to compare one firm's performance to another. Rarely can you make an apples-to-apples comparison. Diversification doesn't come automatically from working with different firms; diversification is in how you allocate the funds.

Historically, when we'd ask a family, "Are we performing similarly to your other advisors?" the answer was, "You're about the same." That's likely because the assets were allocated or split similarly. It's important for clients to understand that they might be invested in the same holdings in two firms, which isn't diversification.

IS YOUR ADVISOR
WHOLESALE OR RETAIL?

When it comes to the cost of working with an advisor, you can ask yourself a key question: Is your advisor wholesale or retail?

Think about taking a trip to Costco versus Walgreens. When you purchase goods at Costco, you get wholesale prices in exchange for buying in bulk. Since the products come straight from the manufacturer and in larger quantities, there are fewer fees incurred throughout the process, and those savings are passed on to you.

Walgreens does have the convenience factor, but prices tend to be higher because there are more middlemen—and thus, more corresponding costs—involved in getting the product from the factory to the pharmacy itself.

Investing in a typical portfolio with a wealth advisor is more like buying retail. Why? Many advisors outsource asset allocation, paying others to do some of the work for them. In those cases, the fees *they* pay are being passed on to you.

We take a wholesale approach, making all portfolio selections ourselves and cutting out added expenses in the process, which allows us to, on average, charge our clients less for our services.

How do you determine whether your current or prospective advisor is wholesale or retail? Simply ask for the complete breakdown of all fees and whether they make the investment decisions in your portfolio themselves. When you do, you'll have more insight into the price you'll pay for their help—and whether those fees will reflect a bargain or a big markup.

Even though it doesn't make sense to pay more fees from a financial perspective, clients often feel more comfortable when they have more than one firm managing their assets. The downside of splitting the assets this way, however, is that it makes coordination more difficult and increases other risks. But the sad truth is that many investors lack trust in the motives of their advisors. This lack of trust stems from traditional advising, where advisors managed as much as possible to accrue as much as possible. The motive wasn't coordination.

Today, the motive behind our approach is the value-saving benefits of coordination. Families preserve wealth and save value overall when a comprehensive plan covers all assets.

TODAY'S 70/30 SPLIT

To help you understand the basis for our approach to risk and value, it's important to highlight what's different about the investment environment of 2020 as opposed to 1979. The big difference can be attributed to what tends to be most people's least favorite topic: interest rates and bonds.

Before you flip ahead to avoid reading anything to do with

interest rates, know that we've tried to make the next few paragraphs as painless as possible. Here goes.

The trend for the past couple of decades has been to keep interest rates as low as possible, with incremental ups and downs. While interest rates may someday rise again to the double digits—the norm of generations past—a climate of low interest rates corresponds with our slightly less conservative approach to investing.

In the past, high interest rates provided families with a simple way to build wealth with "lower risk" assets. For example, we had a client who had a thirty-year US government bond that had just reached maturity. He'd bought it in the 1980s and had a 9 percent return. So when the bond matured thirty years later, he wasn't looking to reinvest in anything more risky than a bond, which had performed well. He wanted to renew and buy another bond. The problem was that bond interest rates were then at 1 percent. Everybody would love a 9 percent bond today, but those no longer exist.

Today's investment climate may require us to take a slightly "riskier" approach, with fewer conservative assets and more "riskier" assets.

In the past, the standard allocation mix was a 60/40 split between aggressive assets and conservative assets—for example, 60 percent stocks, 40 percent bonds. That was a simple rule of thumb to diversify.

In a historically low interest rate environment, we often advise shifting from the traditional 60/40 to a 70/30 split. This is because the current low interest rate environment has made the shift from the traditional 60/40 split to the 70/30 necessary to reach your goals.

But what about all that risk, you ask? How do you account for it?

In chapter 5, we'll show you that not all stocks are exactly alike. By picking less volatile stocks, we can achieve a value similar to the value inherent in the 60/40 split of years past. And we can do so with a similar level of risk over time with more conservative dividend-paying stocks.

The evolving interest rate climate has meant that our general risk tolerance evolved in step. Hence, today's new 70/30 standard. Not too painful, right?

WHAT DO WE MEAN BY COORDINATION?

When coordinating assets, we consider their location, diversification, and concentration. We analyze performance and identify a client's income goals. And then we unify the assets and goals into a single, comprehensive plan.

To create a comprehensive plan, it's essential to map out your expected expenses, then build a family portfolio in a way that generates the income needed in retirement while achieving your other wealth goals. Think about this as we reverse-engineer your income goals to determine the appropriate coordination of investments.

> **Reverse-engineer your income goals to determine the appropriate coordination of investments.**

To accomplish those wealth goals, we'll take into account your outside holdings, all sources of income, such as social security, and the holdings we manage for your family. For clients heading into retirement, a definable income stream is an investment portfolio must-have. Typically, the income is just what's generated from interest and dividends in the portfolio.

Defining your income needs and reverse-engineering your portfolio is the most coordinated, stable approach we know.

Properly coordinating your assets doesn't end there, however. You must also take into account your family members' assets. We see this issue all the time. The matriarch and patriarch complete their estate plan, scheduling times to review and update it. They explain to their children what their wishes are and how they would like their wealth to be stewarded. Everything seems to be buttoned up. But in reality, they haven't taken the next, crucial step: asking how that plan coordinates with those of their children and grandchildren.

It is crucial to understand the nuances of the next generation's financial picture. Why? If you don't understand their circumstances, your decisions about their inheritance could have a detrimental effect on *their* wealth and ability to pass on a meaningful legacy. Some children may be hesitant to share with their parents because they have been more successful than their siblings and might receive less of the future inheritance. We as wealth advisors understand these feelings of uncertainty and can help guide your family proactively.

ALLOCATION AND LOCATION

We like to stress the difference between the *allocation* of your assets and the *location* of your assets.

There are really two types of assets: *retirement* assets, like 401(k)s, and *taxable* assets, like individual accounts, joint accounts, and trust accounts.

There is a divide between those two, necessitating an intentional balancing of each type.

For example: we don't want a client to have $1 million in an IRA and that's it. That can be difficult to manage. Placing all one's wealth into a single asset will likely put stress on income later in life. If that's all the client has, she may find it difficult to generate income when she needs to start taking distributions from that account.

The 70/30 split we mentioned earlier is another example of allocation versus location and the need to rethink conventional wisdom.

Even if you've allocated 70 percent to stocks, we believe it's important to locate assets within investment accounts that benefit from tax-free or tax-deferred growth (for example, Roth IRAs).

Many investors and advisors don't pay attention to the difference between allocation and location. For instance, an aggressive investor might say, "I have $4 million; I want $3.5 million of my money to be invested in growth stocks, and $500,000 to be in bonds." Aggressive approach aside, if he is not paying attention to the titling of where the assets are held, then he isn't doing enough to minimize risk and maximize value.

Back to the retirement assets and taxable assets. As of 2020, when you turn seventy-two years old, you are required to start taking the required minimum distribution, or RMD, from your IRA or, if you are still working, your 401(k). At that point, you must also pay taxes. That could generate an issue for many families, because suddenly they find themselves facing an unexpected burden one year—or over a couple of years—that they hadn't planned for. Suddenly, the retired couple who expected to have a certain amount of income realizes a large portion is now going to taxes, which could mean they are going to receive 30 percent less than they thought they would.

Luckily there are options. Understanding allocation and location helps us find the best option for you and your family.

DIVERSIFICATION AND CONCENTRATION

In our portfolios, we also try not to overweight any particular investment, to strive for diversification. Why? If you end up overly concentrated in any one position and something happens to that investment, you could lose it all.

We'll talk more about diversification in the next chapter, but what's important to note for now is that if you hold a mutual fund—one that encompasses a little bit of everything—you may be overweighted in one particular area but unable to recognize it. For example, say you have a mutual fund that is invested in thirty different companies, one being Apple. You also have an ETF comprised of three companies that overlap with those in the mutual fund, including Apple. Now let's say you also were gifted a hundred shares of—you guessed it—Apple when you were little. What would happen to your portfolio if Apple stock took a downturn? Not only would your hundred shares of Apple stock be affected, but the loss would be compounded, as the ETF and mutual fund would take a hit as well.

By selecting investments on our own, we create a level of transparency that allows us and the family to see the overall diversification at either a micro or macro level. At the micro level we can see the individual stocks or bonds, and at the macro level, we see the overall portfolio balance between all holdings.

CHAPTER 4
LESSONS LEARNED

- **Emotions** can have a big impact on your wealth plan, influencing—for better or worse—the actions you take. Be mindful of how your emotions may lead you to make decisions that could hinder the creation of long-term value. Your wealth advisor should be an important partner in ensuring that the influence of short-term emotions does not interfere with your long-term goals.

- **Coordinating** all your assets under the advice and guidance of one lead wealth advisor can reduce the unintended risk of duplication, uncoordinated tax planning, and misalignment with your true risk profile. Doing so can also reduce your overall fees and the amount of paperwork necessary to effectively manage your financial affairs.

- Coordination of assets also allows your wealth advisor to avoid the risks that can arise from concentrated positions, improve your earning power to meet income needs, and provide better **overall diversification**.

PROMOTING COORDINATION WITH TRANSPARENCY

In chapter 5, Vanessa shows why assets are at risk unless families evolve their understanding of risk, value, and coordinated wealth management. She shares the story of the Daniels family, whose members didn't speak to one another for decades, until they were able to come to terms with their shared financial responsibilities. She explains the four underlying aspects of the FVR approach to asset management, before closing with an appeal to the most important aspect of all: intentional communication.

W e had originally worked with the family patriarch, Mr. Daniels, who passed away almost thirty years ago. As an estate attorney, he had a well-thought-out estate plan and structure in place. After his passing, we helped the family implement the estate plan.

The assets were first transferred into the hands of the mother, but only for her to draw on the income she needed from the portfolio. The rest of the principal was reserved for the kids' benefit. During the financial crisis of 2007 and 2008, one of the sons thought their mother was being a little too aggressive with her investment strategy. As a result, the Daniels family moved their financial accounts to a different firm. At the time, we hadn't yet established a strong relationship with the extended family. We just had a relationship with Ms. Daniels, the matriarch. While we no longer managed her accounts, we remained in touch over the years.

Through her, we heard that two of the sons hadn't spoken a word to one another in twenty-five years. Their conflict originated over some disagreement surrounding their father's passing. Since then, they hadn't even been in the same room together.

Then, a couple of years ago, the Daniels matriarch and her daughter moved their accounts back to us. They hadn't received the results or management care they expected and deserved.

Within the past couple of years, we've been able to help rebuild some of the family relationships. As part of our rebuilding efforts, we recently had a family meeting. It was the first time the whole family had gotten together to talk about the family finances since the big fight. Turns out, it was also the first time that the sons were in a room together since their father passed. From that meeting on, we've been able to make progress in getting all the Daniels family on the same page.

When I say the "same page," I mean literally. The three siblings are trustees of several accounts. It is essential for them to discuss and review the investments together; as trustees they need to make decisions collectively. But for years, they weren't communicating. At first, they couldn't even be included on the same email chain. That's not to say their relationship is perfect today, but the communication has come a long way.

Even though it's been a difficult task for them to adjust, they know it's necessary. It took a lot of encouragement in the beginning, but now they're on the same email chain. We also asked that they attend all the meetings together. So far, so good. They each show up and participate when they need to. It's not our business to know the details of where their dynamics stand when it comes to their personal lives, but from a financial perspective, they can tolerate each other and work together. They've made enough amends to remove the risks their situation had brought to their wealth and estate.

Not only did we help improve communication, but now we're helping them work to build individual wealth plans, ones that also coordinate with that of the larger Daniels family plan.

The Daniels family demonstrates that a degree of transparency and participation by all parties is essential to preserve assets and prevent risks. It's a risk for family members not to talk to one another about their shared finances. If one of them is mostly out of the loop and something were to happen to the assets, it's easy for that one to blame the rest of the family, thinking, *Did I get cheated on my portion of the inheritance?* or *Am I missing something that everyone else already knows?*

> **It's a risk for family members not to talk to one another about their shared finances.**

JR'S TAKE: OUR FAIR VS. EQUAL RECOMMENDATIONS

The Daniels family has three children, and the matriarch and patriarch decided to help each child purchase a home. The parents wanted to give each child 25 percent of the value of the home of their choice in the form of a real estate loan. This can be a nice option to give children a more favorable version of a mortgage. They thought it would be a way to keep things both fair and equal. But they would soon realize that this was easier said than done.

In this family's case, the three siblings also had different income levels. The oldest was divorced and didn't earn nearly as much as the other two. The second was a lawyer, and he brought in a significant income. The third, also a professional, had an income that—when combined with the spouse's income—fell somewhere between the other siblings' income.

As you can imagine, the children chose homes based on the size of their respective incomes. That 25 percent wouldn't be the same for each child. It may have been fair, but it wasn't equal.

When the family was in harmony, this was not an issue. But as soon as the conflict arose between the children, it became a concern.

The issue was compounded by the parents' lack of transparency over the years, which was unfortunate, particularly because the Daniels parents had come up with a solution: they would equalize the amount allocated to each child as part of their inheritance. Things would be fair, *then* equal. But because the overall family estate plan had not been fully communicated, the children's resentment persisted for years.

The siblings wondered if they were receiving their "fair share." And because they didn't have all the information, they just didn't know for sure. Before a parent's passing, it's essential to get the family talking about the estate plan. Doing so can avoid a lot of hurt and angst down the line.

By communicating transparently about "fair versus equal" as part of our approach to managing family wealth, families can avoid hurt feelings and misunderstandings.

Today, all members of the Daniels family have a seat at the table. It's much easier to address any questions as to how the assets will flow. Due to the open discussions, they no longer have the suspicion in the back of their minds that they might not be getting their fair share.

We believe the most transparent way to coordinate a family's wealth is to track all assets on a single document we call the "net worth statement." At the end of this chapter, you'll find a sample net worth statement detailing the Daniels family's assets, as well as a blank sheet for use with your own family.

The net worth statement gives families two big advantages:

1. It allows us to coordinate all your assets, which—as we learned in chapter 4—gives us the opportunity to take a unified approach to items like allocation and location.

2. It shows us all the information on one page, which allows us to analyze real value and real risk more frequently.

When it comes to our approach to a family's assets, we will always seek to minimize risks and maximize value.

In this chapter, we'll help you shift your concept of risk, and we'll share our solutions that offer the most *real* value for families.

THE NET WORTH STATEMENT

The simplest, most comprehensive way to promote coordination is with transparency, and that starts with compiling all your investments onto a one-page net worth statement.

We've learned that a one-page statement is much more powerful than a fifty-page annual review.

Many advisors put together an overfilled document, packed with charts and percentages. We find that few clients ever actually read through or fully understand all these pages. This is not because they are not financial wizards themselves; these documents are quite complicated to discern, even for us—and we are in this business day in and day out.

Moreover, the truth is that a family's most important holdings, risks, and decisions can all be captured in a single document. Why make it any more complicated than that? The simplicity of a net worth statement is a huge relief, in more ways than one.

So, what's in a net worth statement?

Typically, it captures retirement assets, taxable assets, real estate, insurance policies, and private investments. Accounts are only added to the document after we conduct a complete review. For instance, we make sure any insurance policies or estate plans are current before including them in the net worth statement, avoiding multiple layers of complication. The goal is to get a clear understanding of all your holdings onto the page.

With the whole picture in front of us in a format that is easy to understand for everyone involved, we can make the best recommendations possible. This isn't just a surprise for us; it's typically a surprise for families as well, who are finally able to see their overall total.

On many occasions, we've heard a client say, "Oh, I forgot about that asset." Or, "Oh yeah, I guess I did work at three different companies and now have three different 401(k)s that I haven't rolled over."

It may be easy to forget about a 401(k) to which you only contributed $5,000. But if that was twenty years ago, it may have compounded to $40,000 today. For example, we had one client who contributed just a bit every year to a 401(k). She forgot that the company had also participated in profit sharing. After a few good years, she moved on to a different company and left that behind. About fifteen years later as we were building out her net worth statement, she remembered she had an old 401(k). We started the process to track it down and found that the value of the account had continued to compound. By the time we looked at this "forgotten" 401(k), it had $350,000 in it. That's nothing to sneeze at!

As each net worth statement is different for every family, we

> **The bottom line is that with the transparency that a net worth statement provides, we can coordinate your portfolio to minimize risk and maximize value in any investment climate.**

won't elaborate any further on the details. The bottom line is that with the transparency that a net worth statement provides, we can coordinate your portfolio to minimize risk and maximize value in any investment climate. Next, we'll show you how.

OUR TRANSPARENT APPROACH TO MANAGING YOUR ASSETS

When it comes to coordinating your assets to avoid risks, a handful of aspects underpin our approach. The following four aspects highlight how our FVR approach to wealth management differs from the financial industry's status quo approach:

- Prioritizing portfolio income to protect it from risks

- Creating investment transparency

- Engaging in active asset allocation

- Aligning risk tolerance for the right beneficiary

PRIORITIZING PORTFOLIO INCOME TO PROTECT IT FROM RISKS

No matter the investment climate, we've learned, a family preparing for retirement must prioritize *income*. Income is a priority at all ages, whether you are earning your own income with employment or your portfolio is generating it for you. All the asset coordination, transparency, and aspects behind our approach are designed to maximize the value you receive from a portfolio.

Many advisors adhere to conventional wisdom when holding assets. As we've seen earlier, this leads to uncoordinated assets, misallocated wealth, and the risks of tax burdens, lost value, and more. Prioritizing your income needs helps us navigate through the many risks inherent in investing.

With a portfolio focused on income, we coordinate the holdings to maximize your income's cash flow per your goals, while aligning our strategy to meet your level of risk tolerance.

Cash flow comes in many forms, two of which are dividends and interest. The most well-known stream of income is interest generated from bonds. Bonds typically have the most stable stream of income, which is why investors naturally shift their portfolios toward bonds as they near retirement. Our team has an edge in this department since we invest only in individual securities. We are able to generate the desired income stream that our clients are looking for by utilizing both bonds and dividend-paying equities. Companies that have a history of increasing dividends help investors keep up with inflation, whether they are looking for generation of income or building growth.

Some advisors and clients expect stocks or bonds to perform today as they did decades ago. But holding on to the past may not offer the right approach for today's climate, as assets don't always perform the way they have historically. As such, while conventional wisdom from years past may be suggesting you need less risk, today's current environment—complete with low interest rates—may require more risk to reach the same goals.

CREATING INVESTMENT TRANSPARENCY: DO YOU KNOW WHAT YOU OWN?

The new age of investing is automated. Passive investors pick an index matching their risk tolerance and ideally with the lowest fees and let the investment sit for decades. This new way has its merits, mostly in that its inactivity means you can "set it and forget it."

When you invest in an index—say, the S&P 500—you're investing in five hundred of the largest publicly traded companies. You're investing in companies responsible for some of the largest industries: tech, energy, manufacturing, tobacco, firearms, and more. Part of your returns may be coming from the performance of companies that you may not morally agree with—and that may be worth your consideration.

We've had clients who had suffered from cancer or had children who had battled the disease and thus couldn't bear the thought of contributing to a company or industry with known links to cancer.

As gun violence casualties continue to make frequent headlines, we've had meetings with clients who want to make sure they weren't investing in firearms companies. There were some companies that reacted in an unethical manner during COVID-19, and you may not want those in your portfolio. We are able to help clients remove those companies from their portfolios, but that is not the case for those who have their assets managed by advisors who use ETFs and mutual funds.

We had several clients who struggled with outside holdings, such as mutual funds or ETFs. They weren't able to just call their other portfolio advisor and say, "I don't want my funds invested in certain companies." Why? Because the advisor would unfortunately have to admit that those stocks were part of products they didn't actually have control over.

We believe there are many more merits to the original approach, in which a firm picks individual stocks, and the clients are aware of what they own. Knowing what you own and working with advisors responsible for the investments you make is an underlying tenet of our overall philosophy. It's all about transparency—and the confidence and peace of mind that come with transparency.

If our clients ask us to blacklist a particular company, we can do that. I can always show clients exactly what they hold, where it is, and what it's doing.

The trend of being mindful about where your money goes is on the rise. Millennials, especially, are concerned with some of the risks that come with passive index funds. It's important for these investors to put their money where their conscience is. Most firms have a difficult time managing around that. Just look at your holdings, or even just your 401(k). Do you know what you really own?

JR'S TAKE: EXPLAINING THE FINE PRINT

In our business, we read through reams of documents every day. In many of these documents, we see that clients have agreed to and signed things that surprise us. Often when we mention these surprises to the clients, they're equally at a loss.

For example, we might point out, "Hey, did you know that, according to this document, after your second child passes, even if they have descendants, the money will go to your brother?"

"Does it really say that?" many have asked.

Trusts are an example of a binding document with fine print that may turn out to be contrary to your wishes. But we understand how these issues occur: we all have signed something that we didn't fully read. So many of us don't want to take the time to read the fine print, especially if the meter is running.

When we review a client's trusts, we always create a flow chart of the trust's stipulations. The surprises usually surface when we sit down to look over the flow chart one on one with the client.

On many occasions, errors in a trust arise when an attorney only replaces one client's name for another, without making additional changes to the document. If it reads like it was written for another family, it probably was.

This issue is not limited to trusts. We often see problems with annuities, products that clients frequently find themselves locked into, without quite understanding how they got there.

When brokers sell annuities, they often use terminology that differs from what many are used to hearing in their daily lives. Clients may therefore end up buying something that doesn't necessarily work the way they think it does. Even though we do not sell annuities, as part of our holistic review, we walk through the pros and cons with clients, so that they don't find themselves with a case of buyers' remorse later on.

But it's not just about having a team that has your back. As important as it is to work with the right people to prepare your documents and manage your money, it's equally important to always read the fine print and ask questions. We understand that you are busy, which is why we read and explain the fine print in plain English so you can comfortably make a decision.

ENGAGING IN ACTIVE ASSET ALLOCATION

Navigating negative interest rates, or negative yields, is a hot topic in the field today. In this day and age, European investors find themselves essentially paying the bank to hold their money. As we all know, it can be a real challenge to live off negative income.

Those automated low-cost funds that have become the industry norm only contribute to the problem. Investors are at the mercy of the market and its volatility, just hoping things will work out over time. That reality drives home the importance of our approach.

Holding individual fixed-income positions and dividend-paying stocks allows us to provide investors with sustainable income. For example, long-standing companies that raise their dividends regularly serve as fairly secure income streams that families can live on for generations. When selected carefully, and then further diversified with other holdings, these companies offer a sustainable approach that improves overall outcomes.

So if we're not passively investing, what's our approach to active investing? We could write a whole book on the subject, but here's a shorter version that sums it up.

There are two main benefits of active investing that we focus on. First, the ability we have to quickly reposition portfolios to adjust to fluctuations in the sectors they are invested in. For example, during the COVID-19 crash, the dot-com bubble, and the Great Recession, our process allowed us to raise a large percentage of cash to protect but also have the ability to quickly reinvest to not miss out on the recovery. We don't get it right every time, but we get it right over time.

Being able to allocate and reallocate investments from poor performers to good performers, we're able to protect or take advantage of market opportunities. This active approach provides a huge advantage over passive investing.

The second timeless piece we rely on is our cash flow analysis. When you look at the current automation trend in the industry, it's easy to recognize a stark truth: the computer algorithms have a very hard time analyzing cash flow.

Today's technology is phenomenal, with the capability to crunch mind-blowing algorithms. Whether it's the dividend on a stock or the interest payment on a bond, everything that algorithm is investing in is based on the price that a particular security last traded at—whether it's daily, weekly, or monthly. Despite these awe-inspiring developments, automated cash flow analysis is leagues behind in terms of what advisors themselves are capable of.

To help explain, I'll use the example of a real estate investment. If you own a rental building, you may have a vacant unit, so your cash flow might get hit in the short run. But in the long run, if you have good tenants, you can count on that cash flow. The value of the building is based on that overall cash flow—not just the period of time when that unit was empty. The same goes for investing. We don't just think about that short-term vacancy. We think about the unit's overall value based on how it has performed over the years, and that gives us a leg up on automated systems.

When it comes to your individualized portfolio and active investing, asset allocation mobility and cash-flow analysis are the two principal differentiators compared to passive investing.

ALIGNING RISK TOLERANCE FOR THE RIGHT BENEFICIARY

Let's dig a little deeper into our process regarding evaluating risk tolerance with the following hypothetical case.

A matriarch and patriarch at retirement age approached us for help. They have built up a substantial portfolio, which includes funds from a trust the matriarch inherited from her mother.

The matriarch's inherited trust has been invested in stocks for the past fifty years and has grown substantially. This wealth has already been passed on for three generations, and she wants to ensure this continues. Now, though, she is concerned about losing the value of this inherited trust that her mother built. Living through the Great Recession and losing a portion of that wealth has made her nervous, and as a result, she wants to be even more conservative.

Should the trust be invested more conservatively to address her concerns or less conservatively based on the fifty-year time horizon of the ultimate beneficiaries: her grandchildren?

The first step is to identify each of the matriarch and patriarch's financial goals and determine how we could achieve them. One primary goal is to provide the income required for the matriarch and patriarch in retirement. Once that need is covered, we can address what they would like to leave to their children and take steps to make that happen. Building out a legacy and financial plan allows us to have a visual of all the family's goals. With a plan in hand, we are better prepared to address and overcome the matriarch's risk-tolerance concerns.

If we were to separate the wealth the matriarch and patriarch built on their own from the matriarch's inheritance, there would be more than enough for them to live the lifestyle they have become accustomed to and still have money left over.

With that settled, we can focus on the inheritance portion of the portfolio. What should it be invested in? Do we take into account the risk-tolerance concerns of the current matriarch and patriarch when the ultimate beneficiaries of this trust will be the grandchildren—with a time horizon of fifty years or more?

We shared with the matriarch the outcome of our work. After going through this process, it was clear to the matriarch that her inherited trust wasn't needed to meet her income needs or those of her children. She could see that—despite her reservations regarding risk—focusing on growth was appropriate, given the time horizon of the ultimate beneficiaries.

DISCRETIONARY PORTFOLIO MANAGEMENT— WITHOUT THE MIDDLEMEN

As part of our efforts to coordinate a client's assets, we provide a range of services. We believe each service performs best when it's managed by a specialist.

Most firms choose to work with third parties as specialists. These middlemen add multiple layers of cost to a family's portfolio management. There is an explicit fee that comes with bringing in an outside money manager or passive index fund. The other expense comes in the form of opportunity cost. Here's an example: you have a meeting with your advisors. The market is shifting, and you want to reallocate your investments. Your advisor then must contact the third-party manager to process your request to reallocate.

It will take time to execute these trades, creating an inevitable delay in processing that serves as lost-opportunity cost. Now imagine the same client experience, multiplied by the dozens of meetings that occur over the course of a few weeks. Without discretion on the portfolio, the third party can't do anything until instructed to make a move. But if the rebalance recommended by the advisor is so important, it cannot be put on hold until a meeting takes place. Meanwhile, a discretionary manager will execute these trades immediately.

Our investment decisions are made in house, due to our discretionary portfolio management style. We don't outsource any asset management. This is a huge benefit of being an independent firm, one in control of our own outcome.

ABOVE ALL, COMMUNICATION PREVENTS RISKS

We've seen families encounter issues when communication falls apart, as the Daniels family did. When families aren't on the same page, feelings get hurt. When there's little transparency or education, suspicion fills the void. It's only natural. Even worse, those hurt feelings and suspicion can lead to risky decision-making, which can ultimately damage wealth.

This could all be avoided with open and intentional communication.

With the Danielses, the situation was risky because the family members weren't communicating with one another. When the situation was at its worst, the siblings were only talking to their mother.

In the back of their minds, they continued to wonder whether their financial situation was truly fair, compared to that of their other siblings. Since they weren't on the same page, all three siblings suspected they were getting the short end of the stick. With existing issues and angst, you can see how quickly things can spiral. This suspicion would have been further compounded had their mother passed before a conversation was had. Thankfully, as we mentioned, they eventually managed to get on the same page.

We are not sure why the family members were originally at odds with each other, but it was obvious that the financials were just another stressor on their already complex situation. Being open and transparent removed any financial what-ifs that they might have had. They now know what's going on regarding the finances, and they are committed to communicating about them.

Our objective perspective serves as another benefit. We can walk them through various scenarios and act as an unbiased sounding board. That cultivates transparency within the family. From our experience,

> # A little intentional communication goes a long way.

we know transparency can shine a light on risks and promote coordination of assets to eliminate common pitfalls, like a lack of communication, emotional responses to volatility, duplicate fees, tax burdens, and so much more. It can help families prosper. But transparency and coordination can't exist without open communication. At the end of the day, a little intentional communication goes a long way.

CHAPTER 5 TEAR-OFF SHEET

Here is the Daniels family's net worth statement. If you'd like to create your own net worth statement for your family, we've included a template on the next page.

DESCRIPTION	MATRIARCH	PATRIARCH (DECEASED)	OUTSIDE OF ESTATE	TOTAL
INVESTMENT ASSETS				
Retirement Accounts				
· Matriarch IRA - XXXXX392	$ 3,065,000			$ 3,065,000
· Matriarch Roth - XXXXX445	$ 2,137,000			$ 2,137,000
Taxable and/or Tax-Free Accounts				
· Family Trust - XXXXX289			$ 4,216,000	$ 4,216,000
· Marital Trust - XXXXX290			$ 1,387,000	$ 1,387,000
· Partnership - XXXXX560	$ 48,000		$ 3,350,000	$ 3,398,000
· Matriarch Revocable Trust - XXXXX290	$ 2,889,000			$ 2,889,000
· Checking account - XXXXX872	$ 121,000			$ 121,000
Total Investment Assets:	$ 8,260,000	$ -	$ 8,953,000	$ 17,213,000
OTHER ASSETS				
Insurance Products				
· Whole Life Policy			$ 300,000	
· Term Policy			$ 500,000	
Private Investments				
· Investment Property	$ 150,000			$ 150,000
· Start-up Investment	$ 50,000			$ 50,000
Home and Personal Assets				
· Chicago Condo - Home	$ 2,312,000			$ 2,312,000
· California Lake House - Vacation	$ 1,461,000			$ 1,461,000
Total Other Assets:	$ 3,973,000	$ -	$ 800,000	$ 3,973,000
LIABILITIES				
Personal Real Estate Loans				
· Chicago Condo - Residence	$ (628,000)			$ (628,000)
· California Beach House - Vacation	$ (831,000)			$ (831,000)
Other Personal Debt				
· Margin Loan	$ (438,000)		$ (1,134,000)	$ (1,572,000)
Total Liabilities:	$ (1,897,000)	$ -	$ (1,134,000)	$ (3,031,000)
Net Worth:	$ 10,336,000	$ -	$ 10,887,000	$ 18,155,000

_____ Family

Net Worth Statement as of _____

DESCRIPTION	MATRIARCH	PATRIARCH	OUTSIDE OF ESTATE	TOTAL
INVESTMENT ASSETS				
Retirement Accounts				
Taxable and/or Tax-Free Accounts				
Total Investment Assets:				
OTHER ASSETS				
Insurance Products				
Private Investments				
Home and Personal Assets				
Total Other Assets:				
LIABILITIES				
Personal Real Estate Loans				
Other Personal Debt				
Total Liabilities:				
NET WORTH:				

FAMILY LEGACY
AT RISK

In chapter 6, Vanessa returns to the Archer family to share the multigenerational legacy of a lake house. She shows why unintentional conflict and burden pose significant risks to a family's legacy. Vanessa shares how communication, supporting trusts, and gifting are prudent strategies that help avoid potential risks. The chapter closes with a surprising story of a heartbreaking obituary.

When the Archer family's patriarch and matriarch were very young, they bought a lake house as an investment property. When they first bought the lake house, the patriarch and matriarch saw it as a romantic couple's destination. As they didn't have any children early on, they enjoyed using it to escape from city life. Later on, when they had children, the house turned into their family retreat, a place for their five kids to have fun.

Over the years, the lake house became a cherished place for family gatherings. Children, grandchildren, and great-grandchildren grew up there, swimming in summers and sitting fireside together in the winters. What began as an investment became so much more.

The property started off much smaller than it is today. As the Archer family expanded over the years, they slowly bought more land around the original property and continued building. It was a growing property to match the expanding family.

Today, the property is a substantial family compound with a large amount of lakefront real estate. But its most important aspect isn't a pier or a fireplace. It's the fact that this place has been a refuge for the entire family in good times and in bad—helping them overcome a traumatic loss—and this refuge will likely endure long after the patriarch and matriarch are gone.

The lake house was never more important to the family than when the children were young adults and one of the five children passed away unexpectedly. In dealing with the trauma, the family ended up spending most of a summer at the lake house, where they could visit with and help heal one another.

From that summer on, the lake house was a sacred place that would always draw the family close together. Even as the children got married and had their own children, becoming adults who could have chosen to spend their time elsewhere, the lake house remained as important as ever.

When the Archer patriarch and matriarch were in their late sixties, they were pleased the next generation likewise wanted to visit them there. The grandchildren would bring friends, and they all would hang out together, while the grandparents enjoyed hosting and the feeling of being needed. They were pleasantly surprised that younger generations *wanted* to go to Grandma's! Both older and younger generations alike enjoyed the atmosphere.

Today, the grandchildren are either college age or, in many cases, finished with their schooling and raising families of their own. Still, they continue to come together at the lake house each summer.

As mentioned in chapter 2, the Archer family always took an inclusive, multigenerational approach to their assets and estate. They worked together first as a couple, then with their children, to develop a transparent, comprehensive plan that preserved their family's wealth and values.

The lake house, naturally, has been one of the most important pieces of wealth in their plan. It isn't just an asset or a piece of an estate to pass on. It's a legacy of everything that the word "family" means to the Archers. It symbolizes all the joy, sadness, troubles, and love that word represents. What would happen to it once the Archer patriarch and matriarch passed away?

YOUR LEGACY AT RISK

Legacy, when considered as part of a comprehensive wealth plan, can help a family preserve its values and wealth. When *ignored*, legacy can pose serious risks.

Imagine for a moment that the original Archer couple *didn't* have a comprehensive plan in place. What would happen to their wealth, and the legacy of the lake house, when they passed?

Unfortunately, here's one of the most common realities we've seen happen with other families: they struggle with *conflict* and *burden*. Conflict arises when the heirs of a shared property have different financial means and can't agree on how to use and care for the property. Burden can arise when the maintenance and tax obligations of owning a property hit unexpectedly.

Ignoring legacy planning can present a handful of avoidable risks, including:

- conflict among family members and heirs
- tax and maintenance burdens
- lost stories and memories

Many questions arise as well. Who gets to use a property and when, now that the matriarch and patriarch are no longer the ones who decide? Who gives permission? How do you maintain a property and not create conflict and burden for future generations?

Many families don't consider these questions. "It will be an issue for the kids to worry about," the parents might think. But the more you can talk it through prior to the wealth transfer, the better it can work out for family harmony in the long run.

In this case, the family matriarch and patriarch are both running the family business and had five children, four of which will have to continue this lake house legacy. One is an attorney, one is a doctor, one is a teacher, and one still receives support from the matriarch and patriarch. The documents dictate that when the matriarch and patriarch pass on, the four living children must share it.

What happens when the furnace runs out of steam? Or the AC unit breaks down? Or both? Who is responsible for coming up with the money necessary to make repairs if trust money hasn't specifically been designated for property maintenance?

Sure, the four siblings could split expenses equally. But that's less of an option if one of them is living solely off the income they inherited from their parents. As time passes and questions like these pile up, the risk of conflict only increases.

Eventually, one heir might say to another: "You don't make enough money to cover expenses, so you don't get to use the house anymore."

Siblings barring a brother or sister from using a property if he or she can't afford to help cover property expenses is a nightmare situation that, unfortunately, happens time and again. The deceased parents don't live to see the worst of it: what had been a legacy of family unity becomes a source of bitterness and contention.

When it comes to a legacy asset, most think, "My heirs will figure it out. At some point, sure, they'll get angry. But they'll get over it."

Sadly, in many cases, the heirs *don't* get over it. The conflict then creates pain in the family.

Even though scenarios like this one are common, most wealth plans don't account for them.

Typically, an estate plan will note that a legacy asset like a house should stay in the family. In other words, the heirs *shouldn't* sell it and instead should make themselves responsible for its upkeep. That's about the beginning and end of it.

In the Archers' case, there were four individuals in the next generation. With that in mind, when it came to the lake house, the Archers thought through all the little details before they passed.

The Archers asked these questions:

- Is there a document, such as a shared spreadsheet or centralized calendar, showing who spends time at the lake house and when?

- How is time split up? Who gets to have more time and who gets less?

- If something breaks, who has to pay for it?

- What is the process to agree to ever sell the property?

- Is there a supporting trust established with assets that can be used to pay for repairs and maintenance?

- Do the four Archer children share the same burden to keep the property in the family, even though they may be of different financial means?

Based upon our recommendations, the Archers did three things to successfully pass on their legacy: they communicated to prevent conflict and burden, established a supporting trust for the lake house, and embraced gifting to empower the next generation. We'll explain each of these three concepts ahead. First, let's unpack the idea of legacy and how to think of it as you transfer your wealth and values to the next generation.

DO YOUR HEIRS SHARE YOUR PASSION?

As you begin to ask questions and make decisions about what you will pass on, there is one key consideration many overlook. Are your intended heirs as passionate about your assets as you are?

This is particularly important in the case of real estate. Say you have a number of investment properties. Over the years, acquiring them became a passionate project of yours. You spent time lovingly restoring them, finding the right tenants, and making careful decisions about maintenance and repairs.

As a result of your dedication, these properties earned you a substantial sum of money. It's easy to view them as a great investment tool, one your children or grandchildren would be lucky to have. But what if they don't have the same passion for real estate that you do?

Maintaining that type of asset requires so much responsibility and dedication. Without them, the vehicle won't prosper. Instead, it may quickly become a burden, one that won't contribute positively to your legacy in the long run.

Think about what you are planning to leave your heirs. If the asset requires maintenance or special considerations of any sort, your heirs must demonstrate some passion for it. Set up a meeting, and ask them whether it will mean as much to them as it does to you. Their answers should help you determine how to proceed. If no one is interested in maintaining real estate properties after you're gone, perhaps selling those assets before your passing is the right way to go.

Or maybe you had one child in mind to inherit your beautiful artwork that has always had a place of honor in your home. If that child isn't interested in the piece and wouldn't treat it with the same care, perhaps another heir would be better suited to receive it. Or maybe a local art museum or cultural institution should be charged with its continued care.

The reality, though, is that there is no way to know until you ask. If nobody talks about it, there is no way to measure how the next generations will feel. As a result, they may find themselves managing something that is a source of irritation rather than joy.

By the same token, they may be unaware of the emotional and monetary value of what you have passed on, selling it for far below market rate and potentially depriving future generations from a piece of family history.

The only way to avoid a situation like this is to start the conversation. Talk about your plans for your estate, what your various assets mean to you, what they are worth, and how you would like them to be handled after you are gone. Only then can you be sure that you have covered all your bases when it comes to leaving an impactful legacy.

WHAT IS LEGACY?

"LEGACY IS NOT LEAVING SOMETHING *FOR* PEOPLE.
IT'S LEAVING SOMETHING *IN* PEOPLE." —PETER STROPLE

When you are gone, what will remain? What legacy will endure beyond your eventual passing? What will you be remembered for, and who will remember it?

It's essential to think through these questions about legacy as you follow the FVR approach.

Legacy can be a lake house, as in the Archers' case. Or it can be a charitable gift, a set of important values, or even memories and family stories. "Legacy" refers to the beliefs, morals, people, and causes that endure for the benefit of others, even after you're gone.

> When you intentionally establish a legacy for the benefit of others, you help your heirs and beneficiaries sidestep any conflict and burden.

The word "benefit" is key here. When you intentionally establish a legacy for the benefit of others, you help your heirs and beneficiaries sidestep any conflict and burden. You help ensure that your legacy will be remembered in a positive light.

Everyone has a family legacy to pass on. My family legacy has many parts, but one that stands strong is the culture of giving back. We believe that there are traditions that should be kept the same and others that should be improved upon each year. JR's family legacy is living by example, making a difference for future generations, and helping them stay true to our core values. Both JR and I will get into more details in chapter 7.

As we described in the previous chapters on risks to your assets and estate, those to your legacy are similarly affected by a status quo approach to wealth management. When approaching your legacy with purpose as part of your wealth plan, there are three actions to prioritize for your family's wealth and future:

1. Intentionally communicate to prevent conflict and burden

2. Preserve legacy assets with a supporting trust

3. Empower the next generation through gifting strategies

COMMUNICATE TO PREVENT LOST LEGACY

How do you communicate your values to your children and other heirs?

One Saturday morning, I was driving with my daughter Bella, who was seven years old at the time, to help my sister move into her new office. As a psychologist, my sister had just opened her own private practice. Our entire family had marveled at how hard she'd worked in school and throughout her career to get to this point. Opening the office was a big deal for her, as it was for our whole family.

As we drove over, I explained to Bella what we were going to do that day. "We're going to help Auntie Patty set up her office. We're there to help decorate and move stuff around. When we walk in, I want you to tell her you're so proud of her."

"Okay, that's good," she said.

"Aren't you so proud of her?" I asked.

She paused for a moment, and then she said something that surprised me: "Mom, you did the same thing. And I'm proud of both of you."

I blinked, unsure of what she meant for a moment. "I did? How so?"

"You became partner at your firm. And I'm proud of you."

It took me a moment for the words to settle in. In my eyes, yes, I had become a partner of a firm. But I saw that as something different than starting a business from scratch, as my sister has done. After thinking it over, I realized Bella was right. It was the same—an extraordinary accomplishment.

"Yeah, you're right, Mommy did this too," I said. "I'm very lucky to be where I am today."

"No, Mom," she said. "It wasn't luck. You work really hard. You help so many families so that they don't have to worry. And we're all proud of you too."

I tried hard to hold back my tears in the car, because she was right. It took a statement from my seven-year-old for me to reflect on what I had accomplished and to see how what I was doing meant something to our family's next generation.

Many women I know—myself included—tend to attribute success to luck. "Oh, I was lucky. It just happened to work out," we say. But was I lucky enough that my firm picked my résumé and called me? That it worked out and I got the job? That I just happened to get promoted to partner?

"Luck" demeans our achievements, when in reality it is the hard work and dedication that turned a lucky opportunity into an accomplishment. Not explaining the whole story also doesn't allow the next generation to get to know you and all you've done to reach your current station in life. The only thing that does is intentional conversations. Communicate with a purpose, and perhaps your heirs will better understand you—and your wealth.

"You're right again, Bella," I said, smiling now. "I may be lucky, but I definitely worked hard too."

Bella helped remind me how intentional I need to be in communicating my progress and priorities to my family.

Does the next generation understand the work you've done? The life you've built? Do you share with them your struggles and stories? Do you communicate your priorities to them?

When creating an estate plan, it's easy to only discuss the mechanics of wealth transfer. The cold dollar amounts, the faceless accounts, the meaningless assets.

But what about the stories behind the wealth?

When your family understands the work and values you've embraced to achieve success, they'll have a better understanding of the wealth's origin. Understanding an origin helps heirs determine what's best for the wealth's future.

In other words, communicate with the next generation. It's a must.

We've seen too many instances where the next generation, because of a lack of understanding, inherits a legacy that becomes a burden or a trigger to fight. That's unnecessary.

While many families have legacy positions accounted for in their estate plan, most of them don't fully talk about their history. In the absence of conversation, the parents may not understand their adult children's financial picture—and thus which legacy assets would be burdensome and which wouldn't. They may be unaware of any goals the children have. For example, if an heir plans to move away for a new career opportunity, they may prefer to sell off a local real estate asset, rather than maintain it.

The need for open communication of goals and plans, both down to future generations and upward to matriarch and patriarch, are essential. Planning in advance and skipping generations, when it is in the family's best interest, can help with reducing tax risk. This helps prevent an inheritance landing inside an estate that has already reached its maximum estate tax threshold, for instance.

When you talk about such legacy assets, you shine a light on any worries or plans both generations may feel but haven't shared or agreed upon. You can't imagine what a relief it is to have all parties involved when you start talking through the wealth transfer process.

Thanks to our multigenerational relationships with the families we serve, we can help educate the parents as to why they need to communicate legacy intentions effectively by understanding where the children are financially and how to create a plan that accounts for all family dynamics. Once the whole family embraces open communication, solutions for wealth transfer and its impact on all parties become more obvious. Without the proper communication between generations, solving these issues can be an additional challenge.

Let's return to the example of the Archers' lake house. Once we nailed down a plan with the patriarch and matriarch, we had a multigenerational conversation.

In talking through what would happen when the property passes on, we informed the heirs that they would be inheriting the lake house but that they wouldn't have to worry about how they would cover the cost of maintenance or repairs. We shared that their parents had decided to set up a supporting trust that would be used to maintain the property.

Then we walked the four children through a financial statement for the property. The financials included the taxes and regular expenses, like lawn care and utilities. We had also accounted for other yearly expenses that can be easy to overlook, like putting the boat in the dock every year, as well as general updates, because the roof would eventually need to be fixed. These short-term and long-term costs might seem relatively inexpensive, issues that the heirs could sort out when the time came to cross that bridge. But all those items over the course of ten to twenty years add up.

Simply planning to cover those costs by setting up a supporting trust and documenting the plan properly helped set up the Archer legacy for years to come. Then, communicating the intentions from one generation to the next helped seal that legacy, preserving something that could last well into the future.

It was a huge relief for the heirs to understand the specifics and not have to wonder or worry. All the potential struggles and fights that could have occurred in the future seemed to melt away after that one conversation.

The wealthier sibling no longer worried about having to cover those expenses, and those with fewer resources relaxed knowing they wouldn't be on the hook for anything they couldn't afford.

Now that we've covered the role of communication in preserving legacy, let's talk about two financial vehicles many families employ to achieve their goals: supporting trusts, which can help preserve assets like homes, and gifting.

PRESERVE LEGACY ASSETS WITH A SUPPORTING TRUST

It was a huge relief for the younger generations of the Archer family to know the lake house would be kept in the family and cared for with a supporting trust.

As you may have already guessed, a supporting trust allows for your heirs as trustees to cover the administrative costs of a property, paying for its maintenance and taxes with money kept in the trust and used exclusively for the property.

A supporting trust works well for all parties. It allows the trustor to ensure a legacy piece lasts beyond their passing, as the assets in the supporting trust can pay for all costs and its rules can ensure the property will stay in the family.

It also allows the trustees to enjoy the legacy asset and not have to worry about the expenses of its upkeep. In this way, a legacy asset such as a house can be shared without the conflict and burden that can stem from financial responsibility.

As soon as the Archer patriarch and matriarch saw how much the lake house meant to not just their children but also their grandchildren, they set up a supporting trust for the property. Before they passed, they communicated to the trustees—their children—why they set up a supporting trust and how it would work to preserve both the property and family harmony.

Today, both patriarch and matriarch have passed. The next generations still enjoy the lake house. They're deeply grateful they didn't have to sell it and that they have a plan so that all of them will be able to use it fairly. It remains a family retreat, for all the happy and any challenging times to come.

EMPOWER THE NEXT GENERATION: GIFTING WITHIN THE FAMILY

How do you pass on your legacy while you are living?

Many families have discovered that gifting to the next generation can be done in a way that helps strengthen values, without the risks that come with receiving a big lump sum.

What if you'd like to give a grandchild $150,000 in about a decade's time, when you anticipate they may be starting a family of their own? Perhaps if they received this money out of the blue one day, they wouldn't be able to utilize it. We've seen cases where money like that evaporates in a matter of weeks.

But what if you break up that gift into yearly installments of $15,000, starting this year?

Smaller annual gifts allow grand-children to slowly build up their wealth and can help them understand the responsibility and opportunity of the money you're gifting. It allows them to see the good and bad that windfalls can bring and to see it with a smaller dollar

If you've never learned how to handle $15,000, how can you handle $150,000?

amount, rather than risking it all. If you've never learned how to handle $15,000, how can you handle $150,000? Or $3 million?

When we think of legacy, we think of passing on something that benefits the next generations: assets, morals, beliefs, and wisdom.

Gifting today helps you prepare your heirs to receive and manage their inheritance. It allows you to give actual assets now, along with the wisdom and values the family has cherished for generations.

Some people like gifting because it's something their parents or grandparents did for them, and they want to continue the legacy. Some do it for the opposite reason—because it's something their parents or grandparents *didn't* do and they've always wanted to be able to do it for their children and grandchildren.

One of the biggest pieces of advice we like to give, either to people who are beginning to invest or who anticipate receiving an inheritance, is to go out and lose money. It sounds counterintuitive, but it isn't. When we say go out and lose money, we don't truly mean lose it. We want the children to experiment. We all know that making mistakes allows us to learn and adjust accordingly. If you make a bad decision, lose on a $15,000 gift, and learn from it, it'll be a lot better than doing the same with a $3 million inheritance.

To help younger generations benefit from the wisdom and experience you have acquired, you have to avoid having last minute conversations, when it might be too late. Look to pass on your legacy while you are still living. We've seen great legacy and wealth transfer success stories occur when the older generations intentionally prepare the younger ones, especially when gifting within the family.

There are two main types of gifting: *family* and *charitable*.

Family gifting allows you to transfer wealth to your loved ones and to attach values and communication to the wealth being transferred. *Charitable gifting*, meanwhile, allows you to create a positive legacy outside your family by supporting causes and communities and to demonstrate the importance of paying it forward to your heirs. We'll explore charitable gifting in chapter 7, so here let's look at family gifting.

FAMILY GIFTING

Imagine gifting $10,000 to a college-age grandchild. Some families are hesitant to make such a gift, because they don't want to give money right off the bat for fear that their children or grandchildren will spend it on something frivolous. But imagine if this gift were part of your legacy, provided with significant communication about your hopes and intentions for the money and for your heir's future.

With some intention and communication, perhaps they'll use the money responsibly. We've seen many grandparents and grandchildren grow closer as they talk about how to use the funds to reach a life goal. We've also seen grandparents give annual gifts, while the grandchildren receiving them grow more responsible as time goes on.

The gifts can become a fun tradition, a way for generations to bond. They can be a medium to foster a stronger relationship. Those gifts become a conversation piece, an opportunity to pass on stories, values, and wisdom. Many see the gifts as an excuse to meet or talk more often, building additional transparency and communication into their connection. When communication is fostered with smaller gifts, it paves the way for the better management of larger windfalls. Then, when the day comes and the grandchildren become heirs, they approach the windfall with the same responsibility they've learned from those annual gifts.

JR'S TAKE: THE ADDED TAX BENEFIT OF LIFETIME GIFTING

Gifts can come in a variety of forms. You can write a check directly to the recipient or deposit it into a trust for that person's benefit. The decision should be made carefully to ensure that gifting works to the benefit of your unique tax situation.

For example, we often recommend that clients make gifts to trusts rather than directly to the recipient, as the matriarch and patriarch may be more comfortable having the trust own the funds rather than the younger beneficiary. Setting up a "grantor trust" allows you to retain certain powers over the trust and pay the income taxes for the trust. The trust can also receive additional money outside the estate on a tax-free basis and avoid a separate tax return for the trust. If you take advantage of the simple tax-free annual exclusion gifts over many years, the funds can grow substantially outside your taxable estate, providing substantial wealth transfer in the long term.

You can have the trust be a topic of conversation with the younger generation every year when you do your gifting. You can discuss how the investments performed and how even though it may have started with a small amount, with gifting over several years, the amount may be compounded to a few hundred thousand dollars in the trust.

More likely than not, the heirs are going to be better prepared to properly handle that level of wealth and carry on your legacy.

A CAUTIONARY TALE: THE HEARTBREAKING OBITUARY

The Archers ensured their legacy was crystal clear, but that is not always the case. We had a client who told us he was shocked as he read the obituary of a dear friend. He had known the friend for decades and thought he was an extraordinary person with many accomplishments to his name. He couldn't believe the obituary mentioned none of them.

"This is not his legacy. This is not what he was about," he said, shaking his head.

Later on, he learned that his friend's grown children had written the obituary, as is usually the case. So why did the children leave out all their father's remarkable achievements? Our client was surprised to hear it wasn't due to an error or any ill intent—it was just because they had no idea what he had accomplished over the course of his life.

The children lived in other states, saw their father only on holidays, and rarely discussed his work. The obituary showed the extent to which they really knew their father, and it turned out it wasn't much.

Not wanting his friend's legacy to disappear forever, our client met with the children and recapped their father's highlights. He shared the degree to which their father was admired, respected, and accomplished in his community. He shared everything he had, everything that he did, everyone to whom he mattered.

The children were grateful. But they were also sad. It took a friend to tell them this, when it would've meant so much more coming from their own father.

This was likewise an aha moment for our client, who realized he had to make sure he shared his own legacy with his son. He thought, *I'm going to die one day, and I'm going to have an obituary like this if I don't do something about it.*

It's sad to think that his friend is now gone. He didn't share his legacy, which is too often the case. You could be the greatest person in the world, but if your own kids don't know about it, then where's the value in that?

In chapter 7, we'll share how you can lead your family to establish a legacy that lasts. It starts with sharing those stories that mean the most to you—before it's too late.

CHAPTER 6
LESSONS LEARNED

- *Legacy* refers to the things, people, and causes that endure for the benefit of others, even after you're gone.

- Ignoring legacy planning can present a handful of **avoidable risks**, including:
  - conflict among family members and heirs,
  - tax and maintenance burdens, and
  - lost stories and memories.

- **Family gifting during your lifetime** can help nurture and empower the types of wealth guardianship you wish to inspire in subsequent generations. Consider an annual gifting process that includes small yearly installments, such as $15,000, the amount of money that you can give as a gift to one person in any given year without having to pay any gift tax.[4] Smaller yearly gifts (to grandchildren, for example) can help them understand the responsibility and opportunity money provides.

---

4   "Frequently Asked Questions on Gift Taxes," IRS, https://www.irs.gov/businesses/small-businesses-self-employed/frequently-asked-questions-on-gift-taxes#3.

CHAPTER 7

LEAVING A LASTING LEGACY

In chapter 7, JR returns to the Daniels family patriarch, who shielded his children from his story of adversity to the detriment of his own family's legacy. JR shows how to communicate your narrative and use charitable gifting to draw your family closer together. A legacy will last if it is intentionally instilled and communicated, JR notes, before concluding with two stories of family legacy: his own and that of the Archers.

O n a recent Friday afternoon, we met with the Daniels patriarch at his beautiful home in downtown Chicago. While he has been a cherished client for over three decades, in all that time he had never opened up to us about his life. That changed over the course of this meeting, when our scheduled hour turned into three hours, as he shared some of his remarkable story of adversity and subsequent success. And he saved his most heartbreaking reveal for the very end.

As a Jewish kid growing up in a mostly non-Jewish neighborhood, he was treated badly by other kids. Bullying and beatings led to a broken hand that never healed properly and a set of nervous illnesses, such as stomach problems and anxiety, which doctors at the time also had trouble treating.

This sort of adversity would have been too much for most people, but not the soon-to-be Dr. Daniels. He threw himself into his studies and career, working harder than anyone he knew to achieve a better life.

His unyielding perseverance paid off, as he became a respected and successful ophthalmologist. He even pioneered several procedures and devices important in his field, earning a small fortune in the process.

Despite his adulthood success, the bullying, beatings, and religious bigotry he'd endured as a child continued to haunt him, he told us. No matter how much he threw himself into his work, or how respected and successful he became, he struggled to resolve the adversity of his early life.

As he shared his trials and tribulations, Vanessa and I couldn't help choking up—it was clear he had experienced a great deal of pain and had kept these burdens hidden for a long time.

"Have you ever told your kids these stories?" we finally asked.

He shook his head. "No," he said, "I don't want them to feel sorry for me."

"They're not going to feel sorry for you; you're their father," I said. "These are things you can share so they understand how hard it was for you to get where you are today."

In his late eighties, sitting in his large, well-furnished city home, Dr. Daniels would appear to his four children to be that man who woke up every day at 6:00 a.m., worked hard, went to sleep, and became successful throughout the years. They wouldn't know that on top of all that hard work, their father also had to endure horrible treatment at school and in his neighborhood because of his religion and beliefs, that he spent half his childhood doing homework in the hospital, that effects of the abuse lingered throughout adulthood. Lost would be his struggle to fight his past while dedicating himself to a better future.

We thought it was important to share these stories so that his children could understand how much he had overcome to give them the life they had. Kids should be given the opportunity to appreciate where the money comes from and the struggle and perseverance involved to reach that level. They should know that it didn't just fall into Mom and Dad's lap.

Our three-hour conversation was the first of a handful, in which Vanessa and I impressed upon Dr. Daniels how important his stories were to transferring his legacy. Throughout our discussions, we noted how difficult it would be to see him take these stories to his grave, never to be shared.

So, we suggested he write a book—not this book, of course, but his own book, one in which he could share his personal stories with his children. He chose to do so. He agreed to document his experiences, finally telling his life story to his family and creating an heirloom that could be passed on from generation to generation.

We first landed on the idea of a book a few years back when Gene, our firm's late founder, retired from his full-time position. Looking to document his legacy, we discovered a couple of options for sharing your experiences through videos or books. We've since used them with other clients, helping them pass on their stories and values to the next generation.

It's an out-of-the-box idea that most financial advising firms don't suggest, let alone consider. But we've found that it helps solidify our family legacy planning. If you're passing on wealth, there's much more to the process than merely the transfer of money. Think about the degree of wisdom, love, and struggle that it took to create your wealth. For these values to continue on in the next generations, it is equally important to pass on your experiences and wisdom. A book is a practical vehicle to do just that.

Dr. Daniels wrote his book, and he's thankful he did. However, when he finished drafting it, he was at first unsure whether he was going to give this book to his family while he was alive or if he wanted it to be there for them to read after he passed. After giving it more thought, he decided to share his story now, so that his legacy endures. The next generation will be better stewards of his wealth having heard firsthand the stories behind it.

While Vanessa and I advocate strongly for all generations to engage in intentional communication, it is imperative that the senior generations share their legacy with their successors.

A legacy, when passed down hand in hand with financial wealth, helps avoid the risks to family values.

We continue to manage inherited wealth for many children and grandchildren, long after the parents are gone. One day, Vanessa and I visited the child of a client who had recently passed away. He invited us into his home, introduced us to his family, and shared details of the business he'd begun developing since his parents' passing.

Amidst the laughter of grandchildren and the warmth of their home, we saw his success reflected in their joyous family life and in his recent business, which demonstrated impeccable forethought and responsibility.

Having known his parents, we knew they would have been so thrilled to see what we were seeing.

"You know, your parents would be so proud of you," we said.

His answer pleased us: "I know," he said and continued by sharing a story of his parents with us.

Isn't that remarkable? His parents' legacy lived on in his

memory—and would continue in the memory of their grandchildren and beyond. They had successfully passed on a positive legacy and raised children who would remember them for all the right reasons.

The more experience our firm has gained with multiple generations of a family, the more we see how important it is to preserve wealth by incorporating legacy into our financial planning.

When we first began working with families, we focused primarily on addressing their financial goals. But over time, we've become a part of those networks, building long-term relationships. In many cases, we feel as if we're a part of the family too. We hear their stories and listen to situations good and bad. We gain deep insight into each family's dynamics and have learned the ways in which we can offer guidance, both big and small.

Each of us will leave this earth someday. We've been grateful to help the family decision makers to think through their options, so they are in the best position to pass on their story, their legacy, and a chance at a lasting family harmony.

The reality is that every family will face stressors and difficult periods. If those are shared with the next generation, that adversity becomes wisdom. We've seen countless times how grateful the next generation is to hear the truth and how much respect they have for all the experiences of their loved ones.

Whether you make a book or a video or just bring the family together for a conversation or series of get-togethers to intentionally pass on family stories, the effect is the same. It's lasting and positive. You wouldn't believe how this simple act can restore and ensure harmony and likewise preserve your family's wealth.

Throughout the book, we've redefined the status quo approach to financial planning and wealth management. Here, we're redefining legacy.

Many think of legacy as being about themselves—about wanting their own story to endure. But legacy is *always* about the next generation.

Your legacy is about making sure your love is passed on to them. It's about giving them the best possible shot at life. It's not only about living on in their memory—though you very likely will—it's also about giving them the opportunity to have a more solid future by sharing the good and the bad, the wisdom and values behind the wealth. And that is truly priceless.

BUILDING MY FAMILY'S LEGACY

My third child, Rory, was born with a heart condition. At just three months, he had a procedure to correct it. Going through the process, I felt helpless.

I'll never forget what it felt like to have to put my child in the hands of medical professionals, hoping for a positive outcome.

Fortunately, the procedure was a success. Today, Rory is almost six years old, and every day is a reminder of how much he overcame so early in life.

In the midst of it all, though, I met so many other families that felt the same way I did: helpless. The severity of their child's condition dictated much of their lives. Many parents couldn't work, spending most of their waking hours by their child's bedside.

They saw medical bills continue to pile up. And often, as a result, they didn't have the financial flexibility to provide their children with the kind of experience they wanted to offer them during the holiday season.

With that in mind, my family participates in a charity every year around the holidays. We buy gifts for families who have a child struggling with a heart condition and who don't have extra funds to spend on celebrating as a result.

At first, my kids had questions. They wanted to know why we were buying gifts for people we didn't know. I explained what we had been through and what these other families were experiencing. I shared that we were fortunate to have the opportunity to help support them through such a difficult time.

Now, they get excited to pick out gifts each year. They understand that they have the chance to help another family that isn't as fortunate as we were. They understand how powerful it is to be able to help others who have been through a similar situation. Doing so has become part of our family legacy.

DO YOUR KIDS KNOW YOUR STORY?

Do your kids know your story? Do they know how you struggled? The same goes for your own parents' stories. Do you know the intricate details of their personal challenges? Do you know what they went through to get where they are today?

You may have lived with your parents and/or children for much of your life, but you don't necessarily know their personal or professional journey of joy and adversity.

If you're attempting to pass on values and wealth, but you don't share the stories behind them, then you won't fully complete the transfer. The next generation may see the message as being somewhat forced upon them or may not be able to grasp the connection.

But if your heirs can see how your values and wealth are a part of the family history and their stories, it helps explain parts of their lives that they might not have known about otherwise. When the stories are shared, the heirs have a much better appreciation and understanding of those values and wealth.

In working with families, we've found there are several productive ways to pass on the family legacy:

- Telling your story
- Exploring charitable giving
- Connecting generations

TELLING YOUR STORY

The topic of death and end-of-life planning can be difficult, as it can be loaded with fear and grief. Thinking about sharing your legacy can often bring up feelings and behaviors of avoidance in order to sidestep any uncomfortable feelings or situations that stem from a perceived lack of control. But that's just it!

As long as we are living, we still have control over what we want our narrative to be. What we want our lasting memory to be, what we want to pass on to future generations so that they never lose sight of how they got where they are and who the people were who got them there—we control these.

In life, we have a chance to shape our narrative and legacy for our children, our children's children, and beyond. During holidays and celebratory gatherings, when they come across old photos, or when a memory flits through their consciousness on an ordinary Tuesday, our loved ones will talk about us once we're gone. So why not give them the *whole* story of us—the pieces they know and those they don't?

VANESSA'S TAKE: TRANSFERRING LEGACY AND VALUES

How do legacy and values transfer? Do we just have to tell our children to be honest and have integrity, or do we have to show them? I think it's both; you can't just hope they listen to what you have to say or that they are watching you when you are behaving in a manner that reflects your values.

I agree with the saying, "A legacy is caught, not taught," but I believe there is a place for teaching, as well. We live and learn, but in some cases what we experience isn't exactly what we were supposed to learn. I know that sounds a little existential, so let me explain it in another personal story.

In the financial industry, there are many tests that need to be passed in order to practice as an advisor in any particular state. One evening, I was sitting at my dining room table studying. Books and papers were strewn across the table, and I was trying my best to concentrate on the practice exam in front of me. Just then, my daughter came over and drew a rainbow on top of one of my tests.

I was exhausted, hungry, and more than a little frustrated. "Stop touching my things," I told her, before heading off to another area of the house to continue studying.

I didn't think much of the interaction. But the next day, as I was going through my practice exams yet again, I came across that rainbow. I smiled. She was trying to show her support as best she could. In the moment, I had pushed her away, but I didn't have to do that.

It may have seemed insignificant, but exchanges like

that can mean a lot to a child. I knew I had the potential to not only show her the struggles I went through to build my career but also demonstrate that she played a role in keeping me going.

The thing is, our families will tell their version of our story. Our children will remember how a moment like this one played out, as they experienced it. The only way this can be changed is if we intentionally set a goal to intimately share our experiences and insights.

Let's get started on identifying and overcoming our barriers to sharing our personal histories and narratives with our loved ones. Let this be the foundation of our legacy.

There are two factors that can help us share our legacy: responsibility and ritual.

- **Responsibility:** Tell your loved ones that you would like to set a time and date to share with them insights about yourself and your journey. Tell them that you are struggling with avoidance about this and could use the support and accountability to sit down and actually do it. Starting the conversation creates responsibility among both parties, increasing the likelihood that you will accomplish your goal.

- **Ritual:** Create a ritual or tradition around sharing your story. Perhaps you schedule a series of dinners during which you discuss a significant part of your history with your loved ones. That would create an opportunity for engagement while reserving a space to build new memories and establishing a tradition of storytelling—much like our ancestors did.

EXPLORING CHARITABLE GIVING

Legacy is more than just our own personal or professional experiences. It's more than the wealth and wisdom you pass on to your heirs. It's often how we interact with the world.

VANESSA'S LEGACY

My mother was one of ten children born and raised in Guatemala. Coming from a less fortunate family—and faced with days when there wasn't enough food to bring to the table—she told herself if she ever had the means to give back, she would.

When I was ten years old, my family flew to Guatemala to visit my mother's hometown, a small village. We threw a huge celebration just for the village's children, about four hundred kids in total. There were clowns, cake, food, games, music, and more—all the trimmings of a great party.

My sisters, Lesley and Patty, and I were in charge of passing out the food, and then we were allowed to go and play with all the kids. It was the best day ever! Those kids still today call my mother Auntie Alicia. They consider my sisters and me to be their cousins.

I'd like to believe that this act of kindness encouraged some of those children to carry forward the same drive to help others. It definitely has for me; it is very important for me that my daughters are inspired to do the same.

This year, I am sponsoring a teacher in another small village in Guatemala as she works to teach kids how to read. We will be able to formalize this process for years to come, and I will take my girls to help in this process.

Success isn't about how much wealth you have created or about how much you have accomplished. It's about how much you give of yourself to help others.

What if you could fulfill your desire to support worthy causes while nurturing the value of responsible giving in your children and grandchildren?

Here's a scenario we explore with many of our family patriarchs and matriarchs. Let's say you want to give away $100,000 to charity. Rather than just writing a check and calling it a day, perhaps you decide to give your children or grandchildren $20,000 each to designate toward the nonprofit organization of their choice. To make sure their choices are thoughtful, you can have them explain to you why they chose it.

With a little prompting, the next generations see this as the special responsibility it is. We've had many families rally around yearly charitable gifting. Grandchildren will spend weeks exploring different charities or develop a deeper connection with a special one dear to their hearts. It means a lot for the generations to get together and talk about why they believe in a community or cause, and the discussions reinforce their commitment to it.

The next generation doesn't always jump at this opportunity right away. At first, many young people put off the responsibility. Then December rolls around, and they finally get to it. In this case, communication is as important as ever and will pay off over time. The more you talk to the next generation about what's important to them and why, the more likely they are to believe and engage with the value derived from the giving process.

We've worked with many families whose children and grandchild weren't actively involved in gifting in the first few years. Then, after it became an annual tradition, they started to embrace it and look forward to it. Today, the next generation is extremely active. They understand the significance of charitable gifting and view the experience as one of the highlights of their year.

Here is one story. A family set aside a portion of their portfolio for their children to gift. One of their children chose a charity that worked to save animals. The gift the child would make would save the life of one cow. The parents thought it was an unusual choice. They were reluctant to provide a gift for an organization that seemed to have very little impact on the world. But then the child began to explain the rationale behind his choice. As a vegan and someone who cares deeply about animal rights, he wanted to do what he could to protect the life of this animal.

If you are blessed and have set aside a portion of your wealth to give away to help others, why not divide it up and get the next generation involved? While it may be untraditional, it's an opportunity to discover new causes and communities to love and an opportunity to pass on values to your children and grandchildren. We've seen a lot of success come from this approach.

CONNECTING GENERATIONS: DON'T WAIT TO SHARE

Leaving a lasting legacy entails the continuous and intentional communication to connect generations. As mentioned, you don't want to wait until you have an unexpected heart attack and it's too late to share. You also don't want to wait until you're on your deathbed with your pastor, priest, or rabbi at your side, counting on him or her to share your story with your loved ones. That's why it's so important to share your thoughts and beliefs regarding what you would like your family to continue to pass on as a legacy. The added benefit is that it gives you and your family direction. With a legacy plan, you create a path for the family to live by—and you do that by cultivating generational connections.

How can you connect generations? While you may appreciate the opportunity to be the center of attention, it can be challenging for others to sit in a room just listening to story after story. Sharing how your loved ones fit into your story—what they were doing at the time of a particular experience—allows them to feel part of your history too.

For example, if you are telling a story about when you were away at war for three years and sharing specific pain points or accomplish-ments, don't forget to include the fact that your daughter was celebrating her birthday at the time and that having a picture of her blowing out the candles kept you going when you felt you wanted to give up.

> **The earlier you start talking about what's important to you and why, the more likely it is that your legacy will endure.**

It's not the easiest thing in the world to think about your legacy when you're thirty-five years old or to talk about legacy *with* a twenty-five-year-old heir, regardless of your age. But the earlier you start talking about what's important to you and why, the more likely it is that your legacy will endure.

Introducing your desire to share about your personal and family history with your spouse, kids, and grandkids is critical in passing on your legacy. Your stories add richness and texture to your memory and legacy. Your history adds meaning and emotional worth to the material possessions left behind for loved ones.

According to developmental psychologist Erik Erikson, as social beings we develop in stages.[5] In each stage, we struggle with a development "crisis." Perhaps the most relevant to the discussion of legacy is stage seven. Stage seven, Generativity versus Stagnation, suggests that between the ages of forty and sixty-five, we experience a desire to create things that will outlast us; this is generativity. In considering that this urge could be a part of our natural development, shouldn't we take the time to start passing on our legacy, no matter what age or stage we're at in life?

If we could give one piece of advice, it's this: connect with other generations—those that came before and will come after. It's as simple as that.

VANESSA'S TAKE: A TASTE OF OUR OWN MEDICINE

As I was writing this book, a friend called me and asked, "Vanessa, have you talked to your kids about the fact that you're writing a book?" I realized I hadn't!

I was so focused on the process of writing it—*how* to pull it all together—that I had not shared with my children *why* I was writing it.

By not sharing why I had decided to engage in such an undertaking, I had fallen into the same trap I've seen ensnare countless individuals. Let's all please start sharing these

---

5   Saul McLeod, "Erik Erikson's Stages of Psychosocial Development," Simply Psychology, May 3, 2018, https://www.simplypsychology.org/Erik-Erikson.html.

important moments while they happen. This way when you share the memory, it isn't just yours—it's the family's.

We get stuck in the day-to-day. As a result, we don't celebrate big moments and events or the little things that are most important to us. This book is important to me. Thus, even at eight and twelve years old, my children should understand what this book is about and what it means to me to write it.

They may not need to know the complexities of what's inside—the difference between a Traditional IRA and a Roth IRA—but they do need to understand that Mommy has decided to share what she's doing, because she's trying to help other families. Our important stories should be shared with those who are important to us.

As adults, we need to take a step back and remember to share, so that when our kids are grown up, they understand what Mom did and what she believed in and why. That's what keeps our intentions and actions meaningful for the next generation. But it doesn't happen on its own. So, I sat my kids down to have a long conversation, sharing with them why I decided to write this book.

A STORY OF WHAT'S IMPORTANT: JR'S LEGACY

If you're looking to leave a lasting legacy, you should first consider what you're passionate about. We all go through life with day-to-day management of our needs and responsibilities at the forefront of our minds. It's not always easy to uncover our passions. But when a powerful experience brings to light a potential driving force—a reason for being—it's much easier to run with it. Your cause should be close to your heart. In my case, it couldn't be any closer.

If something happens to your children, you can't help but experience a feeling of helplessness. It really doesn't matter if they're newborns, ten years old, twenty, or fifty. You just never lose the connection to your children.

I've already shared that my son was born with a heart defect and that it has had an impact on our family legacy, but I'd like to share a bit more about why the experience was so powerful. We found out about the defect immediately after he was born. Rory was quickly transported from the suburbs of Chicago to a hospital downtown, where he was supposed to have heart surgery within a few days. It turned out his condition was very rare. To increase his odds of success, he was required to go home for three months to grow stronger before the procedure.

During that transitional time, I tried to overcome my feeling of helplessness by researching his condition. I wanted to ensure that we were handling it the best we could and that he had the very best care. I was able to get a second, third, and fourth opinion, searching to find a surgeon with the right experience for his case.

At the same time, we were reassured that our current hospital had identified the right treatment option. Their recommendation was that Rory have a surgery at three months and a later one at five years old. So, while I had found another doctor who could weigh in, I decided to cancel the appointment. I was so overwhelmed by the stress of making the right decision.

Then, the surgeon that I had canceled on, called me. "I know you canceled our appointment," he said, "but please, you should come down to hear what I have to say. I've seen a case similar to what your son has about a year ago. You should come down to listen at least, then decide what is best."

We went, and he explained his potential approach. He said, "You don't do this in two procedures; you do it in one. I'll fix everything in one procedure."

It was difficult. In the middle of a decision—especially one as significant as this—it's easy to second-guess yourself.

We had one of the best hospitals in the country saying they were comfortable doing it in two surgeries. How could somebody do it in one? At some point, though, after taking in all those opinions and feeling every corresponding feeling imaginable, you just have to make a decision.

As soon as we left the meeting, we made up our minds. We put our trust in God and this surgeon who recommended a single, comprehensive surgery for our Rory.

Then came the surgery. There was nothing like the stress of sitting in that hospital, waiting to hear the outcome. As long as I live, I'll never forget the moment the surgeon walked out of the operating room. Thumbs up. We were overcome with relief, experiencing the most profound gratitude. Together, our family went through acute adversity, and in the process gained a deep connection to families going through similar situations and to the medical professionals who help them.

Today, I know more about heart conditions than I would ever want to. But it has become my great privilege to use this knowledge and passion I developed to pay it forward. Today we help other families who, through no fault of their own, are trapped in the same kind of uncertainty.

There are so many parents out there struggling to care for children with heart conditions. About one child in a hundred is born with a heart condition. Some are fairly simple for doctors to treat. Others are so rare that they stump the best medical professionals and put families through incredible turmoil.

Our family made the decision to have this be our lifelong cause. We volunteer in person and support families around the world through our participation in social media groups. We speak at charity events to raise awareness, make donations to support children's heart research, and, of course, purchase gifts for families struggling to manage the financial aspect of such a condition each holiday season. There is a lack of information out there, leaving many families struggling alone and in the dark. We take seriously our responsibility to shine a light for as many families as possible.

This means talking about it with our own family. Our other children can see the scar on their brother's chest, so they ask questions. We explain to them openly and honestly what happened and why today we give back.

As they grow up, they're starting to see how giving back helps build a positive legacy—how it can help other families that went through similar situations. They are very young, but I'm confident they will grow up knowing how to handle tough situations and how to help others through them. I am proud that this will be a part of their legacy too.

THE LEGACY PLAN AND STATEMENT

Building a legacy plan and statement starts with exploring a series of questions:

- What do I believe in?

- How do I want to live my life?

- How can I share this with my family?

- How do I want what I've done to make an impact on other people?

- How can I help others avoid mistakes similar to those I've made and to benefit from what I've done right?

This self-exploration takes a lot of quiet time. You have to sit there and think long and hard. That's why sometimes it's nice to involve other generations in this process. Sometimes you don't know everything you've gone through until people ask about it. When they say, "Hey, did this ever happen to you? How was that? Tell me about when you were in school, the choices you made and why," they provide you with an opportunity to reflect. Reminiscing is so much easier when you have someone to go back and forth with, to help you see the richness of your story.

There is a time and place for everything, including sharing your life stories. We mention in many sections of the book the need for intentional communication. It is necessary to establish a plan in your mind and even on paper with the how and when you will share these stories. Once you have these ideas laid out you can take the next step.

Your legacy statement will look and function a lot like an organization's mission statement. Thinking about your own legacy like a mission statement can be helpful in bringing it to life. You don't need to think of yourself as a charity, but it does help to think about your life within a larger context, as one does when writing a mission statement.

But just because you're attempting to capture your overall message or purpose doesn't mean it has to be long. When creating a legacy statement, some people capture it best with a short, single sentence, while others may have a full page. There is no right and wrong. Your legacy statement just has to be true to who you are.

For example, we have a family whose legacy is summed up in one brief phrase: "honesty and integrity." The family lives by those core values. Whenever a new opportunity arises, whether personal or professional, they apply their core values—honesty and integrity—to determine if and how they should proceed. Using those two values as a stress test keeps them true to themselves—today and tomorrow.

Here's one example of a legacy statement: "*I will follow my intuition and take immediate bold action, because that is the most loving way to proceed. I will only commit to things I can fulfill. I will speak with integrity and reveal my feelings openly and quickly, even if it's uncomfortable at times and may not please everyone. I will only speak about others in a way that would make me comfortable if they were standing in the room.*"

I believe that once you establish your legacy plan, it actually keeps you on track in your life. It is there to remind you of what you believe and what you told yourself in your most honest of moments. That's essential, because, as we all know, it's easy to get off track at times in our lives. Whether we're young or old, we're all at risk of doing things that don't align with our core values.

Talking about and living by the values you establish in your legacy plan and statement will help make sure they

> **The real act of passing on your legacy is continuous communication with your family while you're living.**

last and have the intended effect throughout your life. Keep in mind: The real act of passing on your legacy is continuous communication with your family while you're living.

155

A STORY OF LEGACY: THE GIFT THAT KEEPS ON GIVING

Let's close the chapter by returning to the Archer family. Before they passed, both the matriarch and patriarch created their own books. They also made an effort to communicate their intended legacy to their family. Through their books, legacy statements, and family discussions, they were able to instill important lessons and traditions for the next generation.

The Archers decided that every holiday season they would give a certain amount of money to the next generation, another set amount to the younger generation, and an additional predetermined amount to all spouses and serious partners. They also chose to recognize the modern families within their gifting tradition. If members of their family married individuals with children from a previous marriage, those children received gifts too.

The Archers followed the rules they had established. But would those rules be upheld when they passed away?

You'd think the first rule that could be easily ignored or overlooked would be the gifting to children from a previous marriage. One could rationalize that those children were not a part of the family.

In the Archers' case, a daughter had married a man with three children from a previous relationship. The daughter herself had one child from her previous husband. Since the family managed their holiday gifting tradition through our financial planning process, we were discussing the topic with the daughter one day.

"Will you gift to the three other kids?" Vanessa and I asked.

"Of course," she said. "It's part of our family's tradition. If you're married, then your kids are included, regardless of where they came from. If those children are in committed relationships and living with their partners, they're included too. That's just how we do it."

This wasn't easy for her to do. Her husband had recently passed away, and she was living on a fixed income. It wouldn't be easy for anyone in her situation. We assured her that she was fine and she had enough for herself and gifting to future generations. With our encouragement, she put her nervousness and worries aside and stayed true to her values.

The way she described the family tradition made us so happy. We fondly remembered her parents and were thankful that the legacy they'd established lived on in the next generations. The Archer matriarch and patriarch had stated their legacy, and fully communicated it to their children and grandchildren. Even though they were gone, the family wealth and harmony would endure.

CHAPTER 7 TEAR-OFF SHEET: FAMILY LEGACY STATEMENT

SUGGESTED TIPS:

- Create with no judgement.
- The more vulnerability, the better the communication.
- Don't wait.... You can always update it later with life changes.

HISTORY: TELL YOURS

Family, Childhood, Education, Work Experience

(Example: My parents were not able to continue their higher education, so it was very important for me to continue and succeed, also helping others along the way.)

_____

_____

_____

_____

_____

_____

_____

VALUES: ARTICULATE YOURS

Family, Social, Career, Community, Spiritual

(Example: God and education are two key components of my family values. Another is compassion for others and paying it forward.)

_____

_____

_____

_____

_____

_____

_____

STATEMENT: WRITE YOUR LEGACY STATEMENT

(Example: To improve the lives of current and future generations by providing access to education and mentoring girls to become empowered women.)

_____

_____

_____

_____

_____

_____

_____

_____

CHAPTER 8

CALL TO ACTION

Together, JR and Vanessa present the need for both spouses to become financially literate and for each to play an active role in making decisions for their best future. It may not seem easy to learn the ins and outs of your wealth and how to best manage it, but with a little support, you can become confident about your family's future. The alternative is just too risky. JR and Vanessa both share their take on why and how responding to the call helps families avoid unnecessary risk.

Like many mothers, the Bates family matriarch outlived her husband. As of 2020, she has survived him by more than twenty-five years.

During the first few years after her husband's passing, she "felt lost," which she shared with us in a recent family meeting. Devastated by his passing and bewildered by his financial arrangements, she couldn't make sense of their assets and estate.

While her husband's attorney helped sort through the most urgent matters, he couldn't resolve all the details that her husband hadn't properly smoothed out. "*This* amount didn't have to go to taxes," or "We could have kept *that* insurance policy outside of the estate, rather than in," he'd say, shaking his head.

All told, their attorney estimated that the Bates family parted with hundreds of thousands of dollars that could have been preserved with a little more foresight and coordination.

Never one to let circumstances get the best of her, the Bates matriarch set about educating herself about her family's finances. Within a few years, she achieved mastery over financial jargon and concepts that had once triggered fear and avoidance.

"I did it for my children," she told us in that recent meeting, with great pride. "I vowed they would never be as lost as I was the day their father passed away. That's my legacy."

Her legacy is certainly an admirable one. Over the past fifteen-plus years, she's brought each of her children into the family's financial fold. She's helped them become financially literate and guided them to becoming active participants in the family's wealth, gifting, and legacy decision-making.

Her journey toward values-based family wealth wasn't always easy. As noted in chapter 4, for many years two of her children didn't speak to one another. But despite these ups and downs, she and her children today are at a place where they feel confident in not only their wealth but also their understanding of how to manage it for the present and future harmony of their whole family.

No longer do any of them make decisions in isolation. And this new inclusivity has removed any doubt and suspicions that could have arisen from a lack of transparency. She's led a turnaround for her family. Where her husband had once made all the decisions and kept his family in the dark, today the whole family participates in the process—they are all in the light.

Perhaps the Bates matriarch's most profound legacy is that, when she eventually passes, her children and grandchildren will never experience this kind of confusion resulting from the lack of communication she faced. Due to her thoughtful efforts, those feelings will be replaced with gratitude. The next generation will know what to do, because they are already doing it.

We wrote this book to serve as a call to action for families and the wealth management industry. In this final chapter, we speak directly to our shared need, as family members and industry professionals, to take ownership of the family wealth planning process—and to do it now.

JR'S TAKE: FAMILY VALUE FROM A FATHER'S PERSPECTIVE

Today, we're living in a new world. Just over the past few generations, so much has changed in society. Family dynamics are shifting. In many cases, for the first time, fathers are no longer the primary breadwinners and the exclusive decision makers for their families. This means the way families and the financial industry at large manage wealth should change, as well. We can no longer accept the status quo.

The changes that have come to families are a good thing. In talking with families over the years, we see how many more people are better prepared with the new way than with the old.

The old way typically meant fathers went out, worked, and made money to support the family financially. They traveled for long stretches of time, missing baseball games, ballet recitals, and family dinners. Many fathers we speak with—especially those who are older and at a time in life when they find themselves reflecting on their early years— regret that they weren't around very much for their families during their working years. With the benefit of hindsight, they realize they would like to have been.

Fortunately, today a father's role can be more balanced. Sure, we need to make money and help support the family, but many of us also play an active role in our children's care and upbringing. In many families, this goes hand in hand with mothers playing the role of co- or primary breadwinner. According to the Pew Research Center, in America today, four in ten households have a mother who plays the role of sole or primary breadwinner for her family—a rate that is four times what it was in 1960.[6]

We see now in many households that the overall dynamic and objective is one of mutual balance. Fathers balance working hard with being around to invest time in their children—not just financially, but also by installing their values and sharing their legacy. Mothers balance out childcare responsibilities with their career paths, including roles that were once the domain of men.

If there's anyone holding on to the old way, where patriarchs exclusively made all the decisions and didn't share the information until it was too late, all I can ask is, *Why?*

It's not a leap to see that along with balanced roles and shared family responsibilities, families should create a unified wealth management decision-making and planning process.

As fathers, we've successfully embraced this balance in other parts of our lives. Let's do so when it comes to how we help our family protect its value and manage its wealth.

---

6   Catherine Rampell, "U.S. Women on the Rise as Family Breadwinner," *New York Times*, May 29, 2013, https://www.nytimes.com/2013/05/30/business/economy/women-as-family-breadwinner-on-the-rise-study-says.html.

VANESSA'S TAKE: FAMILY VALUE FROM A MOTHER'S PERSPECTIVE

As mothers, our nature has been to prioritize our spouses and children. We don't talk much about the alternative. This means many of us can feel ashamed for having other priorities or roles, and we tend to experience that ever-present feeling of *mom guilt.* "Am I doing enough for my family? Do I need to be there more? What else can I do?"

We sometimes reach a breaking point. That's because working moms may have a regular job but the work doesn't end there. We still come home to children and have to be "on." There is no time off. There is no, "Let me go home and rest and watch TV for a minute." We have to keep going. We feel that time at home should be quality time with our family. We feel guilty wanting something else.

As mothers operating in a new era, we are still learning individually and collectively how to deal with mom guilt. Getting over this guilt is difficult, because it's so ingrained in our culture.

In the old days, you would hear women tell husbands returning late from work, "I wish you didn't have to work overtime, because then you'd spend more time with us." Or, "I wish you didn't have this obligation, because then we'd be able to do that."

A typical response? "Yes, but I'm working for the family. It's for our overall well-being. I'm doing this so, when we're older, we'll have enough. We'll be covered, and we won't have to worry."

These types of conversations are familiar. The ongoing negotiation is what we're used to. Mothers would agree and demonstrate to their children that it was okay to have to wait for Daddy to come home. When it's the opposite situation—a mother working and a father having more responsibility at home—it's harder for us women to say, "Well, I'm working hard to provide us with the best possible future." It may feel unnatural to your ear. For decades our culture has conditioned us to inherit a legacy of cooking, cleaning, and caring for the kids—and nothing more.

Even though the roles have changed, many mothers struggle to let go of the guilt and still hold on to these old expectations, which makes it difficult to fully embrace the new ones—such as co-leading the family's financial decision-making.

But today's reality is this: Whomever has the opportunity to be a breadwinner can embrace it. It's okay for dads to explain to their kids that they may just have to wait for Mom to come home from a meeting. Each family member should play an active role in coordinating their life together—and that includes the financial decision-making.

This is where we can make a difference as women participating in the family-value planning. We can stand and say, "Back then, you made the money, and I would organize it. Now that we share breadwinning, let's share decision-making too. Let's share responsibility for fully understanding and planning for our family's wealth and future." It doesn't matter who makes more, nor does it matter if only one brings home income, both are creating wealth. This is about sharing experiences and making decisions together. Decisions about your wealth and its future should be made collaboratively for the good of the family and to protect the values of the family wealth.

If you are like many women who say, "Oh, this is way over my head. I just let him deal with it. Just give me the gist of it, and then I'll figure out the rest later," know that you're not alone. You may have been told so many times that as women, we "just won't understand it, so why even bother with it." But that simply is not true—and maintaining that rationale is not helpful to anyone. Today, there just isn't any time for that.

And the truth is, it's not that difficult. You have the ability to sit down and allow a financial professional to explain your finances to you—and it is one of the most important things you can do to protect your family's well-being. We can all let our guard down, be vulnerable, and allow ourselves to learn—and it's always worth our time to do so.

Sharing in the family's breadwinning and decision-making can also be tremendously fulfilling, as you've seen in previous chapters. We've made the case for it throughout this book. Deciding to take action to educate yourself is a big first step, but it's one you can benefit from if you should start today.

Waiting can only lead to more risk. Do it, then help another family member do the same.

If you are in your thirties or forties, for example, and your mom is seventy, and she still has never asked Dad about their financial affairs—now's the time to say, "Hey, Mom, you need to get involved. Let me help you."

We all need support at times. Women need it from other women or men who want to share and help. Everyone has a different personality and benefits from different types of encouragement. Maybe you need that strong daughter by your side who can say, "No, we're going to talk to Dad about this now. We need to get this out in the open. It needs to be shared. We need to understand what happens next."

Don't be embarrassed. Don't be afraid. Don't feel guilty about it. Don't even think twice about asking for help. Everyone is intimidated at the beginning, and it takes time to learn. But the time is now.

Build a comprehensive wealth plan together. Account for your estate, assets, and legacy. Find a wealth management partner you can trust, who understands your family's dynamics and works in all your best interests.

We've repeated our message of inclusivity, transparency, and collaboration throughout the book in many different ways. Now it is your chance to put it to work for your family.

Here at the end, we'll make the case for starting your journey right now, by deciding to take action like Mrs. Bates did after her husband passed. You can become financially literate, starting today.

EMPOWERING OUR CLIENTS TO DEVELOP FINANCIAL LITERACY

To do more for our clients, we make sure to educate them on an ongoing basis. We must all be informed of our options to make the best decision possible for our families and ourselves.

When educating families, we start by sharing our definition of wealth and the ways their family value may be at risk, which we've shared with you in the previous pages.

Redefining wealth within a broader context is the foremost message we share. Why? Because once clients understand our more inclusive, family-oriented approach, we are able to make better decisions together.

To close out our call to action, we'll give you an example of why playing an active role in your financial education is so important.

Recently, JR and I were at a client's housewarming party in Florida. As we socialized, we spoke with a younger couple who asked us about what we do.

When we told them we were wealth advisors, the wife said something we've heard before, yet never fails to surprise us: "Wealth advisors? So that means you get to go on trips all the time, travel the world, check in from the beach—that sort of work?"

In the eyes of many, the typical advisor just makes money off other people's money and does very little actual work.

We were curious to know what gave her that impression. She replied, "Oh, because I follow my advisor on social media, and every other week he's either skiing in Aspen or golfing in Hawaii."

"Okay, so do you call him from time to time to ask what he's doing for you?" we asked.

This seemed to surprise her. "Should I?" she replied. "Typically, we like to wait to go over everything in our annual review."

"What do you go over in your annual review?"

"Well," she said, "we review a document that's at least fifty pages, with figures, lists of percentages, and charts."

"Do you understand it?"

"I don't quite understand every last detail, but my advisor is all over it," she replied.

"He's great," the husband added. "After our last meeting, we walked out feeling like our money has had a great total return year over year."

We've have had many conversations like this. We start by talking investments and returns. By the end, we've gone much deeper to get individuals to understand how their investments connect to their total wealth in a much more holistic, inclusive way. This deeper, more inclusive understanding allows clients to start asking more insightful and purposeful questions for their family and future.

With this couple, Vanessa went deeper by asking something essential that most young people don't consider. "Do you have your wills and trust set up?"

They blinked in surprise. "Even just a simple will is a must-have for every family," she explained. "We've seen countless situations where the family doesn't understand the will's importance until it's too late.

"I know you're young," Vanessa said. "So am I. So is JR. But that doesn't mean any of us can't walk outside and get hit by a car. And in our cases, we all have children. In that situation, what'll happen to your family?"

After about an hour with the couple, we had discussed business assets, college savings accounts, IRAs, building out a net worth statement, charitable aspirations, and potential future gifts—all subjects they'd never spoken about before with their financial advisor.

After a pause, the wife said, "I'm surprised we don't talk about these subjects with our advisor."

While her comments were concerning, they didn't surprise us. Families don't know what to ask sometimes or feel they shouldn't rock the boat. We urge everyone to get help determining if there are any questions they should be asking or concerns they should be focused on. Feel empowered to learn, understand, and take them on.

JR nodded. "We hear that a lot with new clients. But by definition, financial advice should advise on all things financial—for your family, today and tomorrow. Certain situations feel more personal, but if there's money involved, they're financial, too, and that means your advisor can—and should—weigh in. If you're at a car dealership or before you talk with a Realtor. If your parents are in the hospital, or if you're planning for end-of-life care. Because it pertains to your wealth and well-being, your advisor should help guide you in making the most informed decisions to ensure your family's best future."

That conversation was an opportunity for the couple to rethink their approach to wealth, to get ahead of the many risks present in our society's status quo approach.

As an industry and as conscientious family members, we are called now to do better for our futures. Let's answer the call.

CONCLUSION

"Let us not only remember the past and its required
sacrifice, let us also remember that we are responsible to
build a legacy for the generations which follow us."
—Thomas S. Monson

L egacies can vary as much as the families building them do. But
there is a common thread in ensuring their successful con-
struction: building a legacy requires responsibility. You must
make it your responsibility to develop intentional communication
pathways between spouses and generations, in which conversation
flows both ways.

Embracing your responsibility may seem difficult at first, but
once your planning process is on track, you have a better opportunity
to protect your family value from risk.

When spouses share responsibility for and stewardship of the
decisions surrounding a family's overall wealth management, they
tend to make more informed decisions that in the long-term better
serve their well-being and interests.

As we have suggested, including children or any others who will be touched by your wealth and legacy in clear and open financial conversations can be key to successfully passing on your legacy. That approach extends to how we form our client-facing service team: each family is served by an advisor team, which in most cases consists of both a man and a woman, often of different ages to help mirror our clients' multigenerational households. This team structure helps cultivate transparency and inclusivity.

We find that approaching each situation with an inclusive perspective helps us get a full picture of the family dynamics and improves our ability to best serve every family we work with.

Now that you're ready to embark on a journey to protect your family value from risk, you may be wondering about where to start. Here are three main ideas that we've covered in this book that can help direct your planning and conversations:

- Family wealth is more than money

- Collaborative and inclusive wealth planning is key to your success

- Multigenerational conversations create lasting legacies

FAMILY WEALTH IS MORE THAN MONEY

While you and your partner may have organized your financial plans—accounting for all your assets—have you asked yourselves about the morals and values tied to those assets? Are you sure that once those assets pass on to your children and their children, they will understand all it took to acquire them or the responsibility involved in properly managing them? Will they know the aspirations you had for them?

To maintain the wealth you've built, you should be able to answer these questions and more. Think about the meaning of your money and how you'll impart that meaning to your children and grandchildren.

COLLABORATIVE AND INCLUSIVE WEALTH PLANNING IS KEY TO YOUR SUCCESS

To be successful, wealth plans cannot be made in a vacuum. They must be made as a team, which can include matriarch and patriarch, partners, cotrustees, wealth creators, and wealth advisors.

The facilitation of this process should also be a team effort. With this in mind, we have found that the female-male dynamic represented in our advising teams helps support the families we serve and improves outcomes.

From boardroom meetings to family meetings, the world is starting to understand the worth of inclusive behaviors, particularly when it comes to making important decisions. Women and men think differently, and both perspectives add value to the conversation. It's why we need more female advisors and female family members involved in the financial planning process. Collaborative communication will always result in a better, more balanced outcome. In addition to bringing more women into the conversation, we must also make a concerted effort to include other generations.

MULTIGENERATIONAL CONVERSATIONS CREATE LASTING LEGACIES

Picture one of your grandchildren, present or future, speaking from the podium at his graduation. In his speech, he eloquently shares the family's values. Imagine the feelings of pride and accomplishment you would have, watching your grandchild take the first steps to embrace their future and carry on the family legacy.

While we believe that leading by example is crucial to making an impact on younger generations, we have learned that there is much power in having conversations about your family values as well. Having that proud moment of listening to your grandchild's speech will require multiple years of intentional communication, but the payoff is immeasurable.

Of course, the conversation must go both ways. You must also understand where your children and grandchildren are coming from, what their current financial situations are, and what their goals are for the future. Only then can you create a plan that will preserve family value for generations. Having family meetings—a time set aside to share insights both practical and emotional—will allow for that communication to flow both ways: downward to next generations but also upward to the matriarch and patriarch.

FINANCIAL LITERACY: SIMPLIFYING THE COMPLICATED

With those concepts in mind, it's also time to get practical. You can't make progress if you're unsure of how to move forward. No matter your education level or experience, families tend to find themselves somewhat paralyzed when the time comes to make complicated financial decisions. It's bound to happen.

To counteract any complexity, you can simplify as much as possible—but you don't have to do it on your own. A good wealth advisor should distill complex arrangements into a set of simple decisions, while making sure everybody is on the same page. Remember, *everyone* applies to every gender and generation involved. If there is someone whose voice should be heard, make sure to speak up and invite that person to the table.

You can use a few tools to help keep things simple, such as a one-page net worth statement, which we previously described in chapter 5. This single-page net worth statement can be more powerful than the fifty-page, or even hundred-plus-page, documents many advisors typically prepare.

To truly simplify, however, you have to maintain transparency in addition to cultivating financial literacy and keeping things simple.

TAKING ACTION: THREE TOOLS TO HELP PREVENT FAMILY VALUE RISK

In the spirit of simplicity, we'll run through the action steps that merit your attention right away. If you haven't yet utilized the tear-off sheets, we will guide you on which to focus on so that you can start ensuring financial security—and cultivating peace of mind today.

1. Create and/or review your estate plan together

2. Build a family net worth statement

3. Develop your legacy plan

I. CREATE AND/OR REVIEW YOUR ESTATE PLAN TOGETHER

You might feel like everything is okay. But often, that is just because it is easier to say everything is fine than to take action to address your situation. How many times have you been to meetings or parties where people asked, "How are you doing?"

Regardless of how you really feel, our bet is that your typical answer is "Everything is fine." Now, in conversation with a colleague outside your department or at a party with people you may not talk to very often, that may be enough of an answer. But with your wealth advisor, you need to be a little more specific.

There is a serious need to sort through the details. For example, we have demonstrated time and again that life events can and do have an impact on your estate intentions. Knowing what's happening in your head and in your life helps us determine when it's time to review your trust and make updates that could make a tremendous difference in how much your loved ones are set to inherit.

When is the right time to ask your advisor to review your estate plan and tie it into your overall goals? As soon as you complete this book.

And since you've heard our message loud and clear, you know that your spouse should be included first and foremost in the planning. Addressing your estate and legacy plans together makes the process easier when it comes time to share it with the whole family. And when you and your partner are ready to share your plan with your heirs, you'll also have an opportunity to review the precious memories of what you created together.

2. BUILD A FAMILY NET WORTH STATEMENT

Life moves pretty fast these days. There is just too much going on around us to have to remember who you decided to invest money with, what you're investing money in, how many insurance policies you have, the mortgage rates on residential and investment properties, and more. Documenting everything in one place makes keeping track of it all a lot easier.

Hearing this insight, you're likely thinking about completing the family net worth statement in one of two ways:

- Wow, this makes sense. We really need to sit down and fill out this tear-off sheet.

- I don't have that problem, because I don't have all those assets. I'll come back to it when I have more to keep track of.

For those of you thinking you don't have enough to complete a sheet, let alone a fifty-page summary, the truth is you still need this. You still need to keep track of all the financial details in your life. Your 401(k) from work, insurance policies—including those on life, home, and car—and other factors that tend to sit on our minds' back burner all belong on your one-pager.

So, it's time to take action. Go to the end of chapter 5, and start filling out the net worth statement now. You'll feel a sense of relief as soon as it's complete.

3. DEVELOP YOUR LEGACY PLAN

There are many ways to develop your family's legacy plan. We created a short three-step process that can serve as a guide.

First, consider your history. Reminisce about your childhood, life with your parents, your schooling, your career, and your family life. There are many stories that are bound to bubble up, so now will be a good time to write these down.

It is fun to take a look back at everything you've lived through and draw connections between the powerful moments in your life that have shaped you and all that you have achieved. Maybe when you received your first big promotion at work, you were also pregnant with your first baby. Stories like those are wonderful to share with your family; they demonstrate where you came from and what you've been through. These details will help the creation of that legacy plan later on.

The next step is to take an inventory of your values. Here you must think about what experiences have stood out for you as an individual or as a family—and how those experiences have made an imprint on your life and driven your actions. One example is JR's story, in which his youngest son was born with a heart defect and the experience of navigating that challenging time sparked a legacy of giving back. Now he and his family dedicate their time, energy, and financial assets toward raising awareness and helping other families who are going through similar situations.

The final step in this process is to draw connections between what you have noted about your history and the values you have landed upon—complete with the morals, beliefs, and causes that your family cherishes. As we read in Vanessa's story about her daughter pointing out her success and not luck, it is important to communicate wisely and with intention. Make these connections with your children and grandchildren and share the stories in planned-out family meetings. Allow your family to share their thoughts and feelings about what the legacy means to them.

Now you have a plan—you have looked back in time and now know what you want to share, and you have made links to the family. It's family meeting time to share stories and feelings. You can also sometimes find yourself with one or two sentences that can become the family legacy statement. Other times, it can be one to two pages. It all depends on your style; more doesn't mean better and short doesn't mean worse. The whole point is that it addresses your unique circumstances, and those are unlike anyone else's.

TAKING OUR FVR APPROACH OFF THE PAGE AND INTO THE WORLD

In these pages, you've had a chance to gain a better understanding of our FVR, or Family Value at Risk, approach to wealth management. It's our effort to be more inclusive, to account for the entirety of a family's wealth—material and nonmaterial alike—over multiple generations. Over the years, we've seen how our approach helps families make the best possible decisions for themselves and for the family members they have yet to meet.

By now, you understand the importance of focusing on overall wealth returns, rather than just the investment returns. You know that the common practice of limiting one's scope to only those returns on investments (ROIs) and fees doesn't deliver the kind of value most families are looking for. You know that the mainstay of traditional advisors—that the higher the ROI and lower the fee, the better the investment—doesn't always hold up. It fails to capture all the elements that compose a family's full value, which include its assets, estate, and—perhaps most importantly—its legacy.

And now, you have the tools to begin your journey to preserve your family value for yourself, your children, and beyond. If you haven't yet, review the *lessons learned* and *tear-off sheets* at the end of each chapter. And once you have a better understanding of what your family's current wealth picture looks like, consider who can best help you achieve your goals.

A family-value-focused advisory firm helps families look beyond their investment return to focus on the overall wealth return. The priority should be on the family's ability to transfer assets, estate, and legacy so that the value can flow from one generation to the next. By taking this long-term approach, families can avoid the risk of wealth diminishing as it transitions to future generations.

We hope that we have helped you better understand your goals for your estate, assets, and legacy, as well as how best to achieve them. In turn, you have helped us accomplish one of our greatest goals: to share our experience with a wider audience who can benefit from the knowledge we have achieved by guiding families like yours toward the kind of future desired. It is our sincere hope that your family will benefit from these principles for protecting and passing on more of your family's value with less risk. May you close this book not only knowing that there are tools that can help avoid having your family's value at risk, but mainly knowing that the best tool lies within you. Communicate with your family; they want to hear you, and it's your responsibility to share. And if you need a little help, know that we are always here.